CUISINART
FOOD
PROCESSOR
COOKBOOK

Quick and Delicious Dishes for Home Cooks With Modern Appliance

Ben Flatley

©copyright 2024 all right reserved

TABLE OF CONTENT

INTRODUCTION

The best resource for maximizing the capabilities of this multipurpose kitchen tool is the Cuisinart Food Processor Cookbook. This cookbook will revolutionize your culinary experience, regardless of your level of skill in the kitchen or your desire to streamline meal preparation. The food processor is your key to quicker, simpler, and more pleasurable cooking—it's more than simply a device.

Efficiency in the kitchen is crucial in the fast-paced world of today. The purpose of the Cuisinart food processor is to simplify the process of preparing meals. With its ability to chop, slice, shred, & dice food, as well as knead dough and combine sauces, this multipurpose powerhouse drastically cuts down on the time and work required to prepare delectable meals. You may get expert-level accuracy with a single button press, giving you the confidence to experiment with new recipes and cooking methods.

This cookbook provides a selection of dishes that highlight your Cuisinart food processor's limitless potential. From easy weekday meals to decadent sweets and all points in between, there are recipes for every occasion. Learn to prepare dishes like finely cut salads, fresh pesto, creamy soups, smooth hummus, and even handmade dough for bread, pizzas, and pastries. Every recipe is carefully designed to produce tastes that will satisfy even the pickiest palates while making the most of your food processor.

In addition to recipes, this book offers advice on how to get the most out of your Cuisinart food processor. Discover how to set up and maintain your machine correctly, choose the appropriate blades and settings, and solve typical problems. By using this information, you may prolong the life of your equipment and improve your cooking efficiency.

Use the Cuisinart Food Processor Cookbook as a guide to easily prepare tasty, nutritious, and fresh meals. Your Cuisinart food processor is the perfect kitchen partner, whether you're making a gourmet meal or just a fast snack. Accept the ease, improve your cooking, and enjoy each bite of your culinary adventure.

Food Processor Fundamentals

A food processor is a revolutionary tool that goes beyond simple kitchenware. Your Cuisinart food processor is an essential equipment for the following reasons:

❖ **Versatility:**
- Using a single tool, chop, slice, shred, mix, blend, puree, and knead.
- Prepare everything, including the dough for pizza and bread and the finely chopped salad veggies.

❖ **Time-Saving:**
- Reduce the amount of time spent on repetitive chores, such as cutting onions or shredding cheese.
- Your food processor can accomplish it in a matter of seconds, eliminating the need for human work.

❖ **Consistency:**
- Ensure consistent doughs, purees, and cuts each time to give your food a polished appearance.

❖ **Capacity Options:**
- The Cuisinart food processor comes in a range of sizes to suit your culinary requirements, from small to large-capacity bowls.

❖ **Ease of Cleaning:**
- The Cuisinart food processor comes in a range of sizes to suit your culinary requirements, from small to large-capacity bowls.

Essential Attachments and Accessories

There are several accessories for your Cuisinart food processor that are designed to handle certain culinary duties. The most popular attachments and their functions are broken out here:

- **S-Blade (Chopping Blade):** The food processor's central component, perfect for blending, pureeing, and cutting food.
- **Dough Blade:** Ideal for easily kneading dough for bread, pizza, and pastries.
- **Slicing Disc:** It may be adjusted to cut fruits and vegetables into different thicknesses for garnishes, casseroles, and salads.

- **Shredding Disc:** Shreds cheese, carrots, cabbage, and more for recipes like coleslaw or tacos.
- **Grating Disc:** Grates hard ingredients such as Parmesan cheese or chocolate.
- **Mini Work Bowl and Blade:** Ideal for small tasks like chopping herbs, nuts, or garlic without using the full processor.
- **Whisk Attachment (if included):** Whip cream or beat egg whites for desserts and meringues.
- **Citrus Juicer (optional):** Extract fresh juice from oranges, lemons, and limes.
- **Spatula:** Aids in even processing by scraping down the bowl's sides.
- **Storage Case:** Keeps all blades and discs organized and safely stored.

MAPLE CINNAMON BITES

Total Time: 20 minutes | Prep Time: 15 minutes

Ingredients:

1 cup rolled oats

1/2 cup almond flour

1/2 cup dates, pitted

1/4 cup maple syrup

1 tsp cinnamon

1/4 cup almond butter

Pinch of salt

Directions:

1. Pulse almond flour, cinnamon, and oats in a food processor until finely smashed. 2. Put salt, almond butter, dates, maple syrup, and the food processor on high speed. 3. Make a sticky dough by pulsing the ingredients until they come together. 4. Roll little portions of the mixture into balls that are bite-sized. 5. Set the bites in the fridge for 10 minutes after placing them on a parchment-lined baking sheet. 6. You may keep it in the fridge for up to a week if you seal it well. 7. Snack on them for a burst of energy!

FRESH TOMATO SALSA

Total Time: 10 minutes | Prep Time: 10 minutes

Ingredients:

4 ripe tomatoes, quartered

1 small onion, quartered

1 jalapeño, seeds removed

1/2 cup fresh cilantro leaves

1 clove garlic

1 tbsp lime juice

Salt and pepper to taste

Directions:

1. The tomatoes, onion, jalapeño, cilantro, and Garlic should be placed into the food processor of the device. 2. Pulse the contents until they are coarsely chopped and blended with one another. 3. Lime juice should be added, and then salt and pepper should be added to taste. 4. In order to combine, pulse the mixture once more, taking care not to overprocess it. 5. In order to enable the flavors to combine, place the salsa in a bowl and place it in the refrigerator for half an hour. 6. It can be used as a topping for tacos or grilled meats, or it can be served with tortilla chips. 7. The leftovers can be kept in the refrigerator for up to three days if they are stored in an airtight container.

MINT CHOCOLATE BALLS

Total Time: 15 minutes | Prep Time: 10 minutes

Ingredients:

1 cup almonds

1/2 cup dates, pitted

2 tbsp cacao powder

1/4 tsp peppermint extract

1/4 cup shredded coconut (optional for coating)

Directions:

1. To get a finely ground texture, place the almonds in the food processor and pulse them. 2. Use the food processor to incorporate the dates, cacao powder, and peppermint essence. 3. Blend the ingredients together until they come together to make a dough that is sticky and holds together when squeezed. 4. Utilizing your hands, form the dough into bite-sized balls that are modest in size. 5. Should you so wish, you can roll each ball with shredded coconut. 6. To firm up, place it on a platter and place it in the refrigerator for five to ten minutes. 7. This may be refrigerated for a week in an airtight container.

PEPPER JACK CHEESE SAUCE

Total Time: 10 minutes | Prep Time: 5 minutes

Ingredients:

1 ½ cups shredded Pepper Jack cheese

1 cup milk

2 tbsp butter

2 tbsp all-purpose flour

¼ tsp garlic powder   Salt and pepper to taste

Directions:

1. While the pan is on medium heat, melt the butter. To get a smooth mixture, add the flour and whisk constantly for 1 minute. 2. Whisk continuously to prevent lumps as you slowly pour in the milk. 3. Chuck the pepper jack cheese shreds into the mixture once you transfer it to the food processor. 4. The sauce should thicken, and the cheese melts in about a minute or two. Process the mixture. 5. Just a few more seconds in the processor should be enough to mix the garlic powder, salt, and pepper. 6. If you need to reheat the cheese sauce, just pour it back into the pot. 7. Warm it up and use it as a sauce or dip for your favorite foods.

GREEN GODDESS DRESSING

Total Time: 10 minutes | Prep Time: 5 minutes

Ingredients:

1 cup mayonnaise	½ cup sour cream
¼ cup fresh parsley	2 tbsp chopped chives
1 tbsp fresh tarragon	2 tbsp lemon juice
1 clove garlic	Salt and pepper to taste

Directions:

1. To the food processor, add the Garlic, tarragon, chives, and parsley. Chop into tiny pieces by pulsing. 2. Incorporate the mayonnaise, lemon juice, and sour cream into the mixture. 3. After one or two minutes of processing, the ingredients should be completely combined and smooth. 4. Before pulsing to blend, season with salt and pepper to taste. 5. To let the flavors combine, pour the dressing into a jar and set aside to chill for at least half an hour. 6. Dip veggies in it, toss them with salads, or use it as a meat sauce. 7. You may keep any leftovers in the fridge for up to a week.

PUMPKIN SEED PESTO

Total Time: 10 minutes | Prep Time: 5 minutes

Ingredients:

1 cup pumpkin seeds, toasted	1 cup fresh basil leaves
¼ cup grated Parmesan cheese	1 clove garlic
½ cup olive oil	Salt and pepper to taste

Directions:

1. Put the Garlic and roasted pumpkin seeds in the blender. Mince until it resembles a coarse meal. 2. Toss in the Parmesan and basil leaves, and pulse until the cheese is finely minced. 3. Add the olive oil little by little while the machine is running until the mixture is smooth. 4. When you achieve the consistency you wish, stop processing and scrape down the edges if necessary. 5. After a quick pulse to incorporate, season with salt and pepper according to your taste. 6. When ready, keep pesto in a jar in the fridge. 7. Put it on sandwiches, add it to spaghetti, or use it as a dip.

ALMOND JOY ENERGY BALLS

Total Time: 15 minutes | Prep Time: 10 minutes

Ingredients:

1 cup almonds	1 cup shredded coconut
¼ cup cocoa powder	¼ cup honey or maple syrup
1 tbsp coconut oil	½ tsp vanilla extract

Directions:

1. Pulverize the almonds in a food processor. 2. Cocoa powder, honey (or maple syrup), coconut oil, vanilla essence, and shredded coconut should be added. 3. The mixture should be thick and sticky after approximately two or three minutes of processing, pausing to scrape sides as necessary. 4. The dough should be rolled into

balls measuring one inch wide and then placed on a baking sheet. 5. If desired, coat the balls by rolling them in additional crushed coconut. 6. It only needs ten minutes in the fridge at the absolute least. 7. Refrigerate for up to a week if stored in an airtight container.

DARK CHOCOLATE BALLS

Total Time: 15 minutes | Prep Time: 10 minutes

Ingredients:

1 cup pitted dates	1 cup walnuts
2 tbsp cocoa powder	1 tbsp coconut oil
½ tsp vanilla extract	A pinch of salt

Directions:

1. After placing the dates in the food processor, pulse them until they are chopped very finely. 2. Nuts, cocoa powder, coconut oil, vanilla essence, and salt should be added to the mixture. 3. Process the mixture for approximately two to three minutes or until it becomes smooth and begins to clump together. 4. Scoop out the ingredients and roll them into balls that are one inch in diameter. 5. If you want to give the balls an additional coating, you can choose to roll them in cocoa powder or shredded coconut. 6. After placing the balls on a platter, place them in the refrigerator for fifteen minutes so that they may harden. 7. You may keep it in the refrigerator for up to a week if you store it in an airtight container.

COCONUT MATCHA BITES

Total Time: 15 minutes | Prep Time: 10 minutes

Ingredients:

1 cup shredded coconut, unsweetened	1/2 cup almond flour
2 tbsp coconut oil, melted	1-2 tsp matcha powder (adjust for taste)
1-2 tbsp maple syrup or honey	1/4 tsp vanilla extract

Pinch of sea salt

Directions:

1. In a food processor, combine the matcha powder, almond flour, and shredded coconut. Mix everything together by pulsing. 2. Merge the coconut oil, maple syrup, vanilla essence, and a dash of sea salt that has dissolved. The ingredients should be combined until a sticky dough is formed. 3. Make sure it's not too thick by adding additional maple syrup or coconut oil if it's too dry. 4. Form tiny balls with the mixture using a tablespoon. 5. Coat the balls with additional crushed coconut if desired. 6. Allow it to rest in the refrigerator for 10 to 15 minutes before serving. 7. Put any remaining food in the fridge in an airtight container.

BLACK BEAN DIP

Total Time: 10 minutes | Prep Time: 5 minutes

Ingredients:

1 can (15 oz) black beans	1 clove garlic
1 tbsp fresh lime juice	1/4 cup fresh cilantro
1/2 tsp ground cumin	1/4 cup water (adjust for consistency)
Salt and pepper, to taste	

Directions:

1. The black beans, Garlic, lime juice, cilantro, and ground cumin should all be added to the food processor. 2. Maintain a fast processing speed until the components begin to come together. 3. The dip should be gradually diluted with water, a small bit at a time until it achieves the consistency you wish. 4. To mix the ingredients, pulse one more after adding salt and pepper to taste. 5. Transfer the mixture to a dish for serving, and if preferred, garnish it with more cilantro. 6. The tortilla chips or veggie sticks should be served alongside. 7. The refrigerator is

the best place to store leftovers for up to three days.

CREAMY SPINACH DIP

Total Time: 15 minutes | Prep Time: 10 minutes

Ingredients:

1 cup fresh spinach leaves	1/2 cup Greek yogurt
1/4 cup mayonnaise	1/4 cup sour cream
1 clove garlic	1/4 tsp onion powder
Salt and pepper, to taste	

Directions:

1. Put the sour cream, Greek yogurt, mayonnaise, and spinach into the food processor. Proceed to process the ingredients. 2. The Garlic, onion powder, and a dash of salt and pepper should be added at this point. 3. Continue processing until the spinach is chopped very small and the mixture is completely smooth. 4. Test the dip and make any necessary adjustments to the seasoning. 5. Put the mixture on a serving dish and refrigerate for at least 10 minutes before serving. 6. Include a sprinkling of more onion powder or chopped spinach along with the garnish. 7. Serve alongside fresh vegetables, pita bread, or crackers.

ALMOND LEMON CREAM

Total Time: 10 minutes | Prep Time: 10 minutes

Ingredients:

1 cup raw almonds	1/2 cup coconut cream
2 tablespoons lemon juice	1 tablespoon honey or maple syrup
1 teaspoon lemon zest	Pinch of salt

Directions:

1. Take the almonds and place them in the food processor. Blend them until they are completely ground. 2. Coconut cream, lemon juice, honey, lemon zest, and salt should all be added to the food processor. 3. The mixture should be blended on high until it is smooth and creamy, and the sides should be scraped down as necessary. 4. Give it a taste, then make any necessary adjustments to the sweetness or lemon flavor. 5. Transfer the mixture to a bowl once it has been combined, and then place it in the refrigerator for twenty minutes before serving. 6. You may use it as a spread or a dip, or you can add it as a topping to baked goods and sweets. 7. Keep any leftovers in the refrigerator for up to five days if they are stored in an airtight container.

AVOCADO DRESSING

Total Time: 5 minutes | Prep Time: 5 minutes

Ingredients:

1 ripe avocado, pitted and peeled	1/4 cup Greek yogurt
2 tablespoons lime juice	2 tablespoons olive oil
1 garlic clove, minced	Salt and pepper, to taste

Directions:

1. A food processor should be used to combine the avocado, Greek yogurt, lime juice, and Garlic that has been minced. 2. The olive oil, salt, and pepper should be added now. 3. When necessary, scrape down the sides of the bowl as you blend until the mixture is smooth and creamy. 4. To get the desired flavor, adjust the seasoning by adding additional salt, pepper, or lime juice if needed. 5. The dish should be transferred to a serving bowl or stored in a container that is airtight. 6. Make use of it right away as a salad dressing, or refrigerate it for ten to fifteen minutes to achieve a more substantial consistency. 7. You may keep it in the refrigerator for up to three days.

ITALIAN BASIL PESTO

Total Time: 10 minutes | Prep Time: 10 minutes

Ingredients:

2 cups fresh basil leaves	1/2 cup grated Parmesan cheese
1/3 cup pine nuts	1/3 cup olive oil
2 garlic cloves	Salt and pepper, to taste

Directions:

1. Put the Garlic, pine nuts, Garlic, and Parmesan cheese into the food processor. Add the basil leaves. 2. Pulse the ingredients a few times to break them down into smaller pieces. 3. Olive oil should be added in a slow, steady stream while the pesto is being blended until it is completely smooth. 4. A taste is required, and salt and pepper can be added as needed. 5. Repeat the process of blending in order to incorporate the seasoning. 6. The sauce or dip can be used immediately after being transferred to a bowl. 7. To prevent browning, store leftovers in an airtight jar with olive oil.

OATMEAL CRANBERRY BITES

Total Time: 15 minutes | Prep Time: 15 minutes

Ingredients:

1 cup rolled oats	1/2 cup dried cranberries
1/2 cup almond butter	1/4 cup honey or maple syrup
1 teaspoon vanilla extract	1/4 teaspoon cinnamon

Directions:

1. Take the rolled oats and the dried cranberries and put them in the food processor. 2. In order to slightly break down the oats and cranberries, pulse the food processor a few times. 3. Honey, vanilla essence, cinnamon, and almond butter should be added to the food processor by hand. 4. The ingredients should be blended until they form a dough that is somewhat crumbly and sticky. 5. Using your hands, scoop out parts and roll them into balls that are small enough to bite

into. 6. To make the bites more solid, place them on a tray and place them in the refrigerator for ten to fifteen minutes. 7. Place it in an airtight jar and place it in the refrigerator for up to a week.

LEMON BERRY BARS

Total Time: 1 hour | Prep Time: 15 minutes

Ingredients:

1 cup all-purpose flour	1/4 cup granulated sugar
1/4 teaspoon salt	1/2 cup cold butter, cubed
2 large eggs	3/4 cup granulated sugar
1/4 cup lemon juice	Zest of 1 lemon
1/4 cup mixed berries (blueberries, raspberries)	

Directions:

1. Turn the oven on to 350°F, which is 175°C. Line an 8-by-8-inch baking pan with grease. 2. With the help of the food processor, combine the flour, sugar, and salt. 3. Incorporate the butter into the mixture until it becomes the appearance of coarse crumbs. 4. Shape the ingredients into a crust by pressing it into the pan. Just till a little brown, bake for 15 minutes. 5. Eggs, sugar, lemon juice, and zest should be blended until smooth in a separate, clean bowl of a food processor. Add berries and gently mix by hand. 6. Once the crust is done, pour filling over it and return to oven for 20 to 25 minutes more, or until filling is set. 7. After it has cooled entirely in the pan, cut it into bars. 8. Before serving, sprinkle with powdered sugar.

ZESTY LEMON BUTTER

Total Time: 15 minutes | Prep Time: 10 minutes

Ingredients:

1 cup unsalted butter, softened	Zest of 2 lemons

2 tablespoons lemon juice

1 tablespoon honey (optional)

1/4 teaspoon salt

Directions:

1. Put the butter that has been softened into the food processor. 2. Mix in salt, lemon zest, and juice. You can sweeten it with honey. 3. Process until the mixture is silky smooth and creamy, scraping down the sides as necessary. 4. Transfer to a small dish or a container that can seal air out. 5. For the flavors to combine, the dish should be refrigerated for at least an hour. 6. Serve as a spread on pancakes, toast, or scones. Also, great on toast. 7. The remaining food can be kept in the refrigerator for up to two weeks.

ROASTED CAULIFLOWER DIP

Total Time: 35 minutes | Prep Time: 10 minutes

Ingredients:

1 medium head cauliflower, cut into florets	2 tablespoons olive oil
Salt and pepper, to taste	1/4 cup tahini
1 garlic clove	2 tablespoons lemon juice
1/4 teaspoon smoked paprika	

Directions:

1. Heat oven to 400°F (200°C). Olive oil, salt, and pepper should be mixed with cauliflower florets before serving. 2. Roast the cauliflower for twenty to twenty-five minutes until it is soft and golden brown. Spread it out on a baking sheet. 3. Cauliflower should be allowed to cool slightly before being transferred to a food processor. 4. Include smoked paprika, Garlic, lemon juice, and tahini in the mixture. 5. You may need to scrape down the edges of the liquid until it is completely smooth. 6. Adjust the seasoning to your liking. 7.

Pita bread or veggie sticks might be served as an accompaniment.

CRANBERRY RELISH

Total Time: 10 minutes | Prep Time: 5 minutes

Ingredients:

2 cups fresh cranberries	1/2 orange, peeled and seeded
1/2 apple, cored	1/4 cup sugar (adjust to taste)
1 tablespoon orange juice	

Directions:

1. Using the food processor, combine the cranberries, orange, and apple all together. 2. Sugar and orange juice should be added. 3. When the ingredients are coarsely chopped but not puréed, pulse them until they are. 4. To suit your preferences, adjust the amount of sugar in the mixture. 5. Place in a bowl, add a lid, and place in the refrigerator for at least an hour. 6. During the holiday feasts, serve as a condiment or as a side dish. 7. The remaining food can be kept in the refrigerator for up to a week.

TOMATO PEPPER RELISH

Total Time: 15 minutes | Prep Time: 10 minutes

Ingredients:

2 cups cherry tomatoes	1 red bell pepper, seeded and chopped
1/4 red onion	1 clove garlic
1 tablespoon olive oil	Salt and pepper, to taste
1 teaspoon red wine vinegar	

Directions:

1. Chop the cherry tomatoes, bell pepper, red onion, and Garlic till smooth in a food processor. 2. Pulse them to ensure that the components are finely minced. 3. Whisk olive oil, white wine

vinegar, salt, and pepper in a basin. 4. Mix and process for a short period of time; if you want a relish that is chunkier, avoid overprocessing. 5. The seasoning should be tasted and adjusted as required. 6. Move the mixture to a bowl, cover it, and place it in the refrigerator for at least half an hour. 7. Use it as a condiment or as a topping for sandwiches for your sandwich.

CHOCOLATE ALMOND BUTTER BALLS

Total Time: 40 minutes | Prep Time: 15 minutes

Ingredients:

1 cup almond butter	1/4 cup honey or maple syrup
1 cup rolled oats	2 tablespoons cocoa powder
1/2 cup shredded coconut (optional)	1/4 cup dark chocolate chips

Directions:

1. Ingredients like almond butter, honey, oats, and cocoa powder should be added to your Cuisinart Food Processor. 2. Process the mixture until smooth and clumping. 3. After adding the chocolate chips and shredded coconut, pulse the mixture until it is equally distributed. 4. Form the mixture into little balls by scooping out pieces of it and rolling them. 5. Place in the refrigerator for twenty to thirty minutes, or until the mixture is hard, on a baking sheet that has been lined. 6. Put it in the refrigerator in a container that can seal out air.

BOLOGNESE SAUCE

Total Time: 1 hour 30 minutes | Prep Time: 20 minutes

Ingredients:

2 tablespoons olive oil	1 onion, chopped
2 carrots, chopped	2 celery stalks, chopped
1 lb ground beef or pork	1 can (14 oz) crushed tomatoes
1/2 cup milk	Salt and pepper to taste

Directions:

1. A finely chopped onion, carrots, and celery may be achieved with the help of your Cuisinart Food Processor. 2. To prepare the olive oil, heat it in a big saucepan until it reaches a temperature of medium. Proceed to sauté the processed veggies until they have become more tender. 3. Add the ground pork and continue to sauté it until it is browned and the clumps are broken up. 4. Once the crushed tomatoes and milk have been added, stir well. 5. As the sauce thickens, continue to simmer it for one hour while stirring it occasionally. 6. Prior to tossing over spaghetti, season with salt and pepper to taste after seasoning.

MOCHA CASHEW BARS

Total Time: 1 hour | Prep Time: 15 minutes

Ingredients:

1 cup cashews	1 cup dates, pitted
2 tablespoons cocoa powder	1 teaspoon instant coffee powder
1/4 cup dark chocolate chips	

Directions:

1. The cashews should be processed in the Cuisinart Food Processor until they are ground to a fine consistency. 2. After adding dates, cocoa powder, and coffee powder, pulse until sticky. 3. Chocolate chunks should be added and then pulsed to disperse. 4. After lining a baking dish, press the mixture into it. 5. Make sure to refrigerate for thirty to forty minutes. 6. After slicing into bars, place them in the refrigerator.

FRESH MANGO SALSA

Total Time: 10 minutes | Prep Time: 10 minutes

Ingredients:

2 mangoes, peeled and diced	1/4 cup red onion, chopped
1/4 cup cilantro leaves	Juice of 1 lime
Salt to taste	

Directions:

1. While the Cuisinart Food Processor is running, add the mangoes and process them until they are coarsely diced. 2. Toss in with red onion, cilantro, lime juice, and salt. 3. Pulse the ingredients a couple of times to combine them. 4. Add salt, then pulse for a few seconds to blend the ingredients. 5. You may use the mixture as a topping or serve it alongside tortilla chips after transferring it to a bowl.

ALMOND BUTTER FUDGE BARS

Total Time: 1 hour 15 minutes | Prep Time: 15 minutes

Ingredients:

1 cup almond butter	1/4 cup coconut oil, melted
1/4 cup honey or maple syrup	1 teaspoon vanilla extract
1/2 cup almond flour	

Directions:

1. In the Cuisinart Food Processor, combine the following Ingredients: honey, coconut oil, almond butter, and vanilla essence. 2. Keep processing the mixture until it is fully smooth and mixed with the other ingredients. 3. After adding the almond flour, pulse the mixture until it becomes thick and resembles dough. 4. After pressing the mixture into a baking dish that has been lined, smooth the top. 5. Place in the refrigerator for one hour or until the mixture becomes solid. 6. Cut into bars and serve at room temperature.

HAZELNUT MOCHA BALLS

Ingredients:

1 cup roasted hazelnuts	1 cup pitted dates
2 tablespoons cocoa powder	1 tablespoon instant coffee powder
1 tablespoon coconut oil	1 teaspoon vanilla extract
Pinch of salt	

Directions:

1. Put the hazelnuts in your Cuisinart food processor and pulse them until they are completely ground up. 2. To the mixture, add the dates, cocoa powder, coffee powder, vanilla extract, coconut oil, and salt. 3. Process the mixture until it begins to resemble a sticky substance and begins to come together. 4. Take a tiny bit and roll it into balls using your hands. Scoop out the small amount. 5. If you so like, you can roll the balls in chocolate powder or crushed hazelnut chips. 6. Before serving, allow the mixture to refrigerate for fifteen minutes so that it can solidify.

ORANGE COCONUT BARS

Total Time: 40 minutes | Prep Time: 10 minutes

Ingredients:

1 cup shredded coconut	1 cup almond flour
1/4 cup honey or maple syrup	Zest of 1 orange
2 tablespoons orange juice	1/4 cup coconut oil, melted

Directions:

1. In the Cuisinart food processor, blend the almond flour and coconut flour by pulsing them together until they are integrated. 2. Honey, orange zest, orange juice, and coconut oil that has been melted should be added. 3. Process the ingredients until they become sticky and are well

blended. 4. Press the mixture evenly onto a parchment-lined baking dish. Preheat the oven to 350 degrees. 5. Place in the refrigerator for twenty minutes or until the mixture becomes solid. 6. Prepare the bars for serving, and store any leftovers in the refrigerator.

LEMON CAPER SAUCE

Total Time: 10 minutes | Prep Time: 5 minutes

Ingredients:

1/2 cup mayonnaise	2 tablespoons capers, drained
Juice of 1 lemon	1 garlic clove
1 tablespoon fresh parsley	Salt and pepper to taste

Directions:

1. Take the Cuisinart food processor and add the Garlic, lemon juice, capers, and mayonnaise to it. 2. To get a smooth consistency, pulse. 3. After adding the fresh parsley, pulse the mixture until it is almost completely mixed. 4. When seasoning is added, add salt and pepper according to taste. 5. When ready to use, serve immediately or store in the refrigerator.

VELVETY BROCCOLI SOUP

Total Time: 25 minutes | Prep Time: 10 minutes

Ingredients:

1 head of broccoli, chopped	1 small onion, chopped
2 cups vegetable or chicken broth	1/2 cup cream or milk
Salt and pepper to taste	

Directions:

1. While the stock is being brought to a simmer in a saucepan, add the broccoli and onion to the pot. 2. It should take around ten to fifteen minutes for the veggies to become tender. 3. In the event that it is necessary, transfer the mixture to the Cuisinart food processor in stages

and blend it until it is completely smooth. 4. Once the soup has been returned to the stove, mix in the cream. 5. The meat should be served warm after being seasoned with salt and pepper.

HERB-INFUSED MASHED POTATOES

Total Time: 30 minutes | Prep Time: 10 minutes

Ingredients:

4 medium potatoes, peeled and cubed	2 tablespoons butter
1/4 cup milk	1 tablespoon fresh rosemary or thyme leaves
Salt and pepper to taste	

Directions:

1. To make potatoes tender, boil them in a saucepan of salted water for approximately fifteen to twenty minutes. 2. Add the potatoes, along with the butter and milk, to the Cuisinart food processor once they have been drained. 3. Blend till it is silky smooth and creamy. 4. To incorporate the fresh herbs, add them and pulse them briefly. 5. After seasoning with salt and pepper, serve the dish as soon as possible.

CINNAMON RAISIN BARS

Total Time: 40 minutes | Prep Time: 10 minutes

Ingredients:

1 cup rolled oats	1 cup pitted Medjool dates
½ cup raisins	½ cup almond butter
1 tsp cinnamon	Pinch of salt

Directions:

1. Chop the dates, raisins, cinnamon, and oats together in a food processor. 2. The mixture should be blended until it begins to clump together. 3. Pulse the almond butter and salt together until they are completely incorporated. 4. When ready to bake, press the mixture into a

prepared 8-by-8-inch baking dish. 5. After twenty minutes in the refrigerator, cut the mixture into bars. 6. Cool the dish before serving, and store any leftovers in an airtight container.

HAZELNUT COCONUT BARS

Total Time: 35 minutes | Prep Time: 10 minutes

Ingredients:

1 cup hazelnuts	1 cup shredded coconut
½ cup pitted dates	2 tbsp coconut oil, melted
1 tsp vanilla extract	Pinch of salt

Directions:

1. To get a finely ground consistency, grind the hazelnuts in the food processor. 2. Add dates, shredded coconut, coconut oil, vanilla extract, and salt to the mixture. 3. Stir the ingredients together until they come together. 4. Press into a baking dish that is 8 inches by 8 inches and lined. 5. For twenty minutes, chill the mixture in the refrigerator. 6. Bars should be cut into slices and served either cold or at room temperature.

DATE WALNUT BITES

Total Time: 20 minutes | Prep Time: 10 minutes

Ingredients:

1 cup pitted dates	1 cup walnuts
1 tsp vanilla extract	½ tsp cinnamon
Pinch of salt	

Directions:

1. Blend the dates and walnuts together in the food processor after adding them. 2. Mix in the vanilla, cinnamon, and salt, and continue to pulse until a sticky dough is formed. 3. Use your hands to roll the mixture into little balls. 4. Put the bits on a tray lined with parchment paper. 5. Chill for ten minutes so that it can become more solid. 6. You may eat them as snacks after storing them in an airtight container.

STRAWBERRY SHORTCAKE BALLS

Total Time: 25 minutes | Prep Time: 10 minutes

Ingredients:

1 cup freeze-dried strawberries	1 cup cashews
½ cup shredded coconut	2 tbsp honey or maple syrup
½ tsp vanilla extract	

Directions:

1. Cashews and freeze-dried strawberries should be processed until they are fine. 2. Blend in the shredded coconut, honey, and vanilla extract until everything is incorporated. 3. Form the mixture into little balls and set them on a pan that has been lined. 4. 15 minutes should be spent chilling in the refrigerator. 5. Before serving, place any leftovers in the refrigerator.

CINNAMON ALMOND BALLS

Total Time: 20 minutes | Prep Time: 10 minutes

Ingredients:

1 cup almonds	1 cup pitted dates
1 tsp cinnamon	½ tsp vanilla extract
Pinch of salt	

Directions:

1. Until the almonds are finely crushed, process them. 2. Mix in the dates, cinnamon, vanilla extract, and salt until the mixture becomes sticky. 3. Form the mixture into balls and place them on a lined tray. 4. Place in the refrigerator for ten minutes to set. 5. Relish it or put it away in a sealed container.

HAZELNUT DATE BALLS

Total Time: 25 minutes | Prep Time: 10 minutes

Ingredients:

1 cup hazelnuts	1 cup pitted dates

2 tbsp cocoa powder

1 tbsp coconut oil, melted

Pinch of salt

Directions:

1. Through the use of a food processor, the hazelnuts should be processed until they are entirely ground. 2. Include salt, dates, cocoa powder, and coconut oil in the mixture. 3. Repeat until the mixture becomes sticky, amending with oil as necessary. 4. Once the mixture has been rolled into balls, lay them on parchment paper. 5. Chill for fifteen minutes in the refrigerator. 6. Serve the leftovers, and then put them away in a container.

CHAI COCONUT BALLS

Total Time: 20 minutes | Prep Time: 15 minutes

Ingredients:

1 cup unsweetened shredded coconut	1 cup almonds
1/2 cup pitted dates	2 tsp chai spice blend (or a mix of cinnamon, cardamom, ginger, and cloves)
1 tbsp coconut oil	1 tbsp honey or maple syrup
1/4 tsp sea salt	

Directions:

1. After placing the almonds in the food processor, pulse them until they are coarsely chopped but not completely crushed. 2. Dates, coconut, chai spices, salt, and coconut oil should be added if desired. Blend until everything is well blended. 3. The mixture should be blended until it forms clumps, and then honey or maple syrup should be drizzled in. 4. Using a firm pressing motion, shape the mixture into balls measuring one inch in diameter. 5. For the purpose of coating, roll the balls in additional shredded coconut. 6. Before serving, place in the refrigerator for at least ten minutes to allow the

ingredients to set. 7. Place it in an airtight jar and place it in the refrigerator for up to a week.

CASHEW CHIA BALLS

Total Time: 15 minutes | Prep Time: 10 minutes

Ingredients:

1 cup raw cashews	1/2 cup pitted dates
2 tbsp chia seeds	1 tbsp almond butter
1 tbsp honey or maple syrup	1/2 tsp vanilla extract
1/4 tsp sea salt	

Directions:

1. The cashews should be placed in the food processor and pulsed until they are minced very coarsely. 2. Dates, chia seeds, almond butter, honey, vanilla extract, and salt should be added. 3. The ingredients should be blended until they form a sticky dough. 4. Prepare the mixture by scooping it out and shaping it into little balls. 5. If you so wish, you can roll each ball in additional chia seeds. 6. Prepare the dish by placing it in the refrigerator for a minimum of five minutes. 7. Put it in the refrigerator in a container that can seal out air.

MOCHA CASHEW BALLS

Total Time: 15 minutes | Prep Time: 10 minutes

Ingredients:

1 cup raw cashews	1/2 cup pitted dates
1 tbsp cocoa powder	1 tsp instant coffee granules
1 tbsp coconut oil	1 tbsp maple syrup or honey
1/4 tsp sea salt	

Directions:

1. Process the cashews in the food processor until they are totally smashed. 2. Dates, cocoa powder, coffee granules, salt, and coconut oil should be added to the mixture. 3. It is necessary to process the mixture until it starts to clump

together. 4. Maple syrup should be drizzled in, and the mixture should be blended until a sticky dough is formed. 5. The ingredients should be rolled into little balls. 6. In the event that you so wish, roll each ball in extra chocolate powder. 7. Before serving, let the dish chill in the refrigerator for at least ten minutes.

MAPLE PUMPKIN BALLS

Total Time: 20 minutes | Prep Time: 15 minutes

Ingredients:

1/2 cup pumpkin puree	1 cup rolled oats
1/2 cup pitted dates	1/4 cup almond butter
1 tbsp maple syrup	1/2 tsp cinnamon
1/4 tsp nutmeg	1/4 tsp sea salt

Directions:

1. After placing the oats in the food processor, pulse them until they are completely ground. 2. Dates, pumpkin puree, almond butter, maple syrup, cinnamon, nutmeg, and salt should be then added to the mixture. 3. In a blender, process the ingredients until they achieve a creamy consistency and begin to clump together. 4. Assemble the ingredients into balls with a diameter of approximately one inch. 5. Should you so want, you can roll each ball in more ground oats or cinnamon. 6. Put the mixture in the refrigerator for at least ten minutes so that it can solidify. 7. Put it in the refrigerator in a container that can seal out air.

PECAN FUDGE BALLS

Total Time: 15 minutes | Prep Time: 10 minutes

Ingredients:

1 cup raw pecans	1/2 cup pitted dates
2 tbsp cocoa powder	1 tbsp almond butter
1 tbsp honey or maple syrup	1/2 tsp vanilla extract
1/4 tsp sea salt	

Directions:

1. The pecans should be pulsed in the food processor until they are coarsely chopped. 2. Dates, cocoa powder, almond butter, honey, vanilla extract, and salt should be added together. 3. The ingredients should be blended until they form a sticky dough. 4. The mixture should be scooped out and then rolled into little balls. 5. In the event that you so wish, you can roll each ball in extra cocoa powder or crushed pecans. 6. Put in the refrigerator for at least five minutes to cool before serving. 7. Ensure that the container is sealed and place it in the refrigerator.

DILL PICKLE DIP

Total Time: 10 minutes | Prep Time: 10 minutes

Ingredients:

1 cup sour cream or Greek yogurt	1/2 cup cream cheese, softened
1/2 cup chopped dill pickles	1 tbsp pickle juice
1 tbsp fresh dill, chopped	1/2 tsp garlic powder
Salt and pepper to taste	

Directions:

1. Smoothly combine sour cream and cream cheese in a food processor. 2. Toss in some chopped pickles alongside their juice, some dill, garlic powder, salt, and pepper. 3. Perform a few pulses until the pickles are dispersed equally throughout the mixture. 4. The mixture should be transferred to a serving bowl, and extra dill should be sprinkled on top. 5. If you want the flavors to come together, refrigerate the dish for half an hour before serving it with chips or vegetables. 6. Any necessary adjustments to the seasoning should be made before serving. 7. In an airtight container, leftovers can be refrigerated for three days.

CARROT GINGER VINAIGRETTE

Total Time: 10 minutes | Prep Time: 10 minutes

Ingredients:

1 cup carrots, chopped	2 tablespoons fresh ginger, peeled and sliced
1 garlic clove	¼ cup rice vinegar
¼ cup soy sauce	2 tablespoons sesame oil
¼ cup vegetable oil	1 tablespoon honey or maple syrup
Salt and pepper to taste	

Directions:

1. Carrots, ginger, and Garlic should be mixed together in the food processor bowl. Pulse until extremely finely minced. 2. Add the soy sauce, rice vinegar, and sesame oil to the mixture. Blend until it is completely smooth. 3. Emulsify the mixture by gradually adding vegetable oil while the machine is operating. 4. Begin by adding honey, and then season it to taste with salt and pepper. 5. Puree till it is silky, smooth, and creamy. If it is required, adjust the seasoning. 6. You may use it as a dipping sauce for vegetables or as a topping for salads. 7. You may keep it in the refrigerator for up to a week if you store it in an airtight bag.

CRANBERRY ALMOND BARS

Total Time: 40 minutes | Prep Time: 15 minutes

Ingredients:

1 cup almond flour	½ cup oats
⅓ cup coconut oil, melted	⅓ cup honey or maple syrup
1 teaspoon vanilla extract	1 cup dried cranberries
¼ cup slivered almonds	

Directions:

1. Put the oven on to a temperature of 175 degrees Celsius (350 degrees Fahrenheit). 2. Using parchment paper, line a baking pan that is 8 inches by 8 inches. 3. Mix oats and almond flour in a food processor until combined. 4. Coconut oil that has been heated, as well as honey and vanilla essence, should be added and processed until a dough is formed. 5. Using a gently pulsing motion, incorporate the cranberries and almonds into the mixture without over-processing it. 6. Evenly press the mixture into the pan that has been prepared. 7. Cook for twenty to twenty-five minutes or until the edges are golden. 8. Once the bars have completely cooled, they may be cut into bars and served.

PEANUT BUTTER AND JELLY BARS

Total Time: 45 minutes | Prep Time: 15 minutes

Ingredients:

1 cup rolled oats	1 cup whole-wheat flour
½ cup peanut butter	¼ cup honey
½ cup butter softened	1 teaspoon vanilla extract
½ cup fruit jam of choice (strawberry or grape)	

Directions:

1. Preheat oven to 175°C (350°F). 2. Using parchment paper, line a baking pan that is 8 inches by 8 inches. 3. In the food processor, grind the oats until they are very finely ground. 4. Process the ingredients until a dough is formed, adding the flour, peanut butter, honey, butter that has been melted, and vanilla. 5. In the pan that has been prepared, press half of the dough. 6. On top of the dough layer, spread jam in a uniform layer. 7. Crush the remaining dough and sprinkle it on top of the jam layer. 8. Take the

bars out of the oven when they have cooled for 25–30 minutes.

COCONUT CHOCOLATE BARS

Total Time: 30 minutes + chilling time | Prep Time: 10 minutes

Ingredients:

1½ cups shredded coconut	½ cup coconut oil, melted
¼ cup maple syrup	1 teaspoon vanilla extract
1 cup dark chocolate chips	

Directions:

1. Food processor the shredded coconut until it clumps. Add the vanilla extract, maple syrup, and coconut oil, and mix until everything is thoroughly blended. 2. Put the mixture into a pan that is 8 inches by 8 inches and lined with parchment paper. 3. Make chocolate chips smooth in the microwave or double boiler. 4. After the chocolate has melted, pour it over the coconut mixture and smooth it out evenly. 5. Place in the refrigerator for one to two hours or until the mixture becomes solid. 6. In order to serve, cut into bars.

CHOCO-DATE BALLS

Total Time: 15 minutes | Prep Time: 15 minutes

Ingredients:

1 cup pitted dates	½ cup almonds
¼ cup cocoa powder	2 tablespoons almond butter or peanut butter
1 teaspoon vanilla extract	Pinch of sea salt
Shredded coconut or cocoa powder (for rolling)	

Directions:

1. Mince the almonds by pulsing them in a food processor. 2. Turn the mixture into a sticky consistency by adding the dates, cocoa powder, almond butter, vanilla, and salt. Process until combined. 3. Form little balls out of the mixture using your hands. 4. Coat each ball by rolling it in either additional cocoa powder or shredded coconut. 5. Put the balls on a platter and let them firm up in the fridge for about 15 to 20 minutes. 6. You may keep it in the fridge for up to a week if you seal it well. 7. Try it as a sweet treat or nutritious nibble.

HERB BALSAMIC VINAIGRETTE

Total Time: 10 minutes | Prep Time: 5 minutes

Ingredients:

1/2 cup extra-virgin olive oil	1/4 cup balsamic vinegar
1 clove garlic, minced	1 tablespoon Dijon mustard
1 teaspoon honey	1/4 teaspoon salt
1/4 teaspoon black pepper	1 tablespoon fresh basil, chopped
1 tablespoon fresh parsley, chopped	1 tablespoon fresh thyme leaves

Directions:

1. Balsamic vinegar, Dijon mustard, honey, salt, pepper, and Garlic should all be added to the food processor bowl. 2. Mix everything together at a low speed in a processor. 3. Emulsify the olive oil while the processor is running by carefully adding it via the feed tube. 4. For the dressing, add the basil, parsley, and thyme and pulse a few times to combine the herbs. 5. Reevaluate the seasoning according to your taste. Transfer to a storage container and keep in the fridge for a week.

SPICY CASHEW DRESSING

Total Time: 15 minutes | Prep Time: 10 minutes

Ingredients:

1/2 cup raw cashews, soaked	1/4 cup water (adjust for desired thickness)
1 tablespoon soy sauce or tamari	1 tablespoon rice vinegar
1 tablespoon lime juice	1 clove garlic, minced
1 teaspoon sriracha (or more, to taste)	1 teaspoon honey or maple syrup
Salt and pepper, to taste	

Directions:

1. Following the process of draining the cashews that have been soaked, place them in a food processor along with water, soy sauce, rice vinegar, lime juice, Garlic, and sriracha. 2. Run the blender on high until the mixture is completely smooth and creamy. 3. Combine the honey, salt, and pepper by pulsing the ingredients together. 4. It is important to taste the seasoning and make any necessary adjustments by adding additional water. 5. The dressing should be transferred to a container and stored in the refrigerator for up to five days.

FRESH PICO DE GALLO

Total Time: 10 minutes | Prep Time: 10 minutes

Ingredients:

4 ripe tomatoes, seeded and diced	1/2 small red onion, chopped
1 jalapeño pepper, seeded and finely chopped	1/4 cup fresh cilantro, chopped
Juice of 1 lime	Salt, to taste
Freshly ground black pepper, to taste	

Directions:

1. The bowl of the food processor should be filled with tomatoes, red onion, jalapeño, and cilantro leaves. 2. Pulse the ingredients a few times until they are just blended but still have some chunks. 3. The ingredients should be combined by pulsing them once or twice, and then the lime juice, salt, and pepper should be added. 4. Test the seasoning, then make any required adjustments. 5. Immediately serve or store in the refrigerator for up to three days.

ALMOND JOY ENERGY BARS

Total Time: 20 minutes (plus chilling time) | Prep Time: 10 minutes

Ingredients:

1 cup almonds	1 cup pitted Medjool dates
1/2 cup unsweetened shredded coconut	2 tablespoons cocoa powder
1/4 teaspoon salt	2 tablespoons coconut oil, melted

Directions:

1. The almonds should be pulsed in a food processor until they are finely minced. 2. Put in some dates, some shredded coconut, some cocoa powder, and some salt. The mixture should be processed until it starts to come together. 3. While the food processor is operating, slowly drip in the heated coconut oil until it is completely integrated. 4. To make an even layer, transfer the mixture to a small baking dish coated with parchment paper and firmly press down. 5. Wait one hour for the mixture to become hard, then cut it into bars and enjoy it. You may keep it in the refrigerator for up to a week if you store it in an airtight container.

SWEET AND SPICY CHILI SAUCE

Total Time: 20 minutes | Prep Time: 5 minutes

Ingredients:

3 red chili peppers, seeded and chopped	2 cloves garlic, peeled
1-inch piece fresh ginger, peeled	½ cup rice vinegar
¾ cup sugar	½ cup water

1 tablespoon
cornstarch

Directions:

1. Chop some garlic and ginger and throw them into your Cuisinart food processor. Chop into tiny pieces by pulsing. 2. Transfer the contents to a saucepan and combine with the sugar, water, and rice vinegar, stirring constantly. Combine by stirring. 3. Over medium heat, whisk the ingredients until they boil. 4. After it comes to a boil, thicken it with the cornstarch slurry. 5. Keep heating, stirring often, until the sauce thickens, which should take around 5 minutes. 6. Once cooled, add to a jar; remove from heat. 7. Keeps for up to two weeks when refrigerated.

CINNAMON HAZELNUT BITES

Total Time: 15 minutes | Prep Time: 5 minutes

Ingredients:

1 cup hazelnuts, toasted	1 cup pitted dates
½ cup shredded coconut	1 teaspoon cinnamon
1 tablespoon maple syrup	Pinch of salt

Directions:

1. Chop the hazelnuts coarsely by pulsing them in a food processor. 2. Sea salt, dates, coconut, cinnamon, maple syrup, and stir. 3. Mix on high until dough forms small clumps and stays put when squeezed. 4. Use your hands to roll little amounts into balls. 5. Coat the bites with additional crushed coconut if you like. 6. After 10 minutes in the fridge, transfer to a dish and set aside to harden. 7. Refrigerate for up to seven days if stored in an airtight container.

LEMON POPPYSEED BALLS

Total Time: 15 minutes | Prep Time: 5 minutes

Ingredients:

1 cup almonds	1 cup dried apricots
Zest of 1 lemon	2 tablespoons lemon juice
1 tablespoon poppy seeds	1 tablespoon honey

Directions:

1. Toss the almonds into the food processor and pulse until they are coarsely minced. 2. Come up with a mixture of honey, poppy seeds, lemon zest, lemon juice, and dried apricots. 3. Mix until a sticky, clumpy consistency is achieved. 4. Form little balls out of the mixture by scooping it. 5. Roll the balls in extra poppy seeds if you want to decorate them. 6. After 10 minutes in the fridge, transfer to a dish and set aside to harden. 7. Refrigerate for up to seven days if stored in an airtight container.

SMOKY CHIPOTLE DIP

Total Time: 10 minutes | Prep Time: 5 minutes

Ingredients:

1 cup sour cream	½ cup mayonnaise
1 chipotle pepper in adobo sauce	1 teaspoon smoked paprika
1 clove garlic, minced	Salt and pepper to taste
Fresh cilantro for garnish (optional)	

Directions:

1. Mixed with chipotle pepper, sour cream, and mayonnaise in a Cuisinart food processor. 2. Blend in the smoked paprika and minced garlic with a few pulses until everything is smooth. 3. Sprinkle salt and pepper on top or adjust the amount as needed. 4. Place in a bowl and serve. 5. If you like, you may top it off with some chopped fresh cilantro. 6. To let the flavors meld, chill it in the fridge for 15 minutes. Alternatively, you may serve it immediately. 7. Serve with tortilla chips or sliced fresh vegetables as a dip.

CHOCOLATE HAZELNUT SPREAD

Total Time: 25 minutes | Prep Time: 10 minutes

Ingredients:

2 cups hazelnuts	1 cup dark chocolate chips
2 tbsp cocoa powder	1 tbsp coconut oil
1/2 cup powdered sugar	1/2 tsp vanilla extract
1/4 tsp salt	

Directions:

1. Turn the oven on to 350°F, which is 175°C. After laying out on a baking sheet, roast the hazelnuts for 10 to 12 minutes. 2. Peel hazelnuts by rubbing them with a towel once they have cooled. 3. Cream the hazelnuts in a food processor for approximately 5 minutes or until they are completely smooth. 4. Bring the chocolate chips and coconut oil to a boil in a double boiler or microwave-safe bowl. 5. Blend the hazelnut paste with the melted chocolate, cocoa powder, powdered sugar, vanilla extract, and salt. Puree the mixture. 6. Put it in a jar and put it somewhere cool to keep it.

CILANTRO PEPITA PESTO

Total Time: 10 minutes | Prep Time: 5 minutes

Ingredients:

2 cups fresh cilantro leaves	1/3 cup pepitas (pumpkin seeds)
1/3 cup grated Parmesan cheese	2 cloves garlic, peeled
1/2 cup olive oil	Juice of 1 lime
Salt and pepper to taste	

Directions:

1. The food processor should be stocked with garlic, cilantro, pepitas, and Parmesan cheese. 2. Pulse until extremely finely minced. 3. While processing, add olive oil in a slow and steady stream until it is completely smooth. 4. Mixing lime juice, salt, and pepper together should be done in order to achieve the desired flavor. 5. Take a taste, and make any necessary adjustments to the seasoning. 6. You may serve it or put it in an airtight refrigerator container.

MATCHA ENERGY BALLS

Total Time: 15 minutes | Prep Time: 5 minutes

Ingredients:

1 cup pitted Medjool dates	1/2 cup almonds
1/4 cup cashews	1 tbsp matcha powder
1 tbsp chia seeds	1 tbsp coconut oil

Directions:

1. The food processor should be filled with cashews, dates, and almonds. Pulse until the mixture is coarsely minced. 2. Include matcha powder, chia seeds, and coconut oil in the mixture. 3. Continue to blend until the mixture becomes cohesive and sticky. 4. Form the mixture into balls by scooping out amounts that are the size of a tablespoon. 5. For an additional option, you may roll the balls in shredded coconut or more matcha powder. 6. The refrigerator is the best place to store it for up to a week.

GREEN OLIVE TAPENADE

Total Time: 10 minutes | Prep Time: 5 minutes

Ingredients:

1 cup pitted green olives	1 clove garlic
1 tbsp capers	1/4 cup fresh parsley
2 tbsp olive oil	Juice of 1/2 lemon
Salt and pepper to taste	

Directions:

1. Add the olives, garlic, capers, and parsley to the food processor and pulse until smooth. 2. To roughly chop, pulse the ingredients. 3. Combine

the lemon juice and olive oil by pulsing the ingredients together. 4. Salt and pepper should be used to taste, and salt should be used to season. 5. Pulse the ingredients until they achieve the required consistency. 6. Accompany the dish with crackers or bread.

CAESAR SALAD DRESSING

Total Time: 10 minutes | Prep Time: 5 minutes

Ingredients:

1/2 cup mayonnaise	1/4 cup grated Parmesan cheese
1 tbsp lemon juice	1 tsp Dijon mustard
1 clove garlic, minced	1/2 tsp Worcestershire sauce
Salt and pepper to taste	

Directions:

1. Utilize the food processor to include the following Ingredients: mayonnaise, Parmesan, lemon juice, mustard, garlic, and Worcestershire sauce. 2. Puree till it is silky, smooth, and creamy. 3. Salt and pepper should be added to taste, depending on the situation. 4. Transfer to a container or jar for storage. 5. Immediately use or store in the refrigerator for up to a week. 6. Before serving, take a stir.

SPINACH ARTICHOKE DIP

Total Time: 20 minutes | Prep Time: 10 minutes

Ingredients:

1 cup fresh spinach, packed	1 cup canned artichoke hearts
1 cup cream cheese	½ cup sour cream
½ cup grated Parmesan cheese	½ cup shredded mozzarella
1 garlic clove, minced	Salt and pepper to taste

Directions:

1. Arrange the artichokes and spinach in the food processor bowl. To roughly chop, pulse the ingredients. 2. Cream cheese, sour cream, Parmesan cheese, mozzarella cheese, garlic, chili pepper, and salt should be added. 3. Process the ingredients at a high speed until they become creamy and smooth. 4. After pouring the mixture onto a baking dish, smooth it out evenly. 5. Bake until bubbly at 350°F (175°C) for 10 minutes. 6. After a further two to three minutes under the broiler, brown the top. 7. Served hot with chips, bread, or vegetables might be served.

JALAPEÑO RANCH DIP

Total Time: 15 minutes | Prep Time: 10 minutes

Ingredients:

1 cup sour cream	½ cup mayonnaise
1 jalapeño, seeded and chopped	1 garlic clove
½ cup fresh cilantro leaves	1 tablespoon fresh lime juice
Salt and pepper to taste	

Directions:

1. It is recommended to incorporate sour cream, mayonnaise, jalapeño, garlic, and cilantro into the food processor. 2. A few food processor pulses break down the ingredients. 3. Add salt, pepper, and lime juice. 4. Blend on high until creamy and silky. 5. Take a taste, and make any necessary adjustments to the seasoning. 6. Place the mixture in a bowl, cover it, and place it in the refrigerator for five minutes so that it may thicken. 7. As a spread, serve with chips, vegetables, or as a snack.

CREAMY POTATO SALAD

Total Time: 30 minutes | Prep Time: 15 minutes

Ingredients:

4 medium potatoes, peeled and cubed	½ cup mayonnaise

¼ cup sour cream

2 tablespoons Dijon mustard

1 celery stalk, chopped

1 green onion, sliced

Salt and pepper to taste

Directions:

1. Cook potatoes in salted water for 10 minutes, drain, and cool. 2. Add the mustard, sour cream, and mayonnaise to the food processor and pulse until smooth. Blend until it is completely smooth. 3. Pulse the celery and green onion until they are completely incorporated. 4. Mix in potatoes that have been allowed to cool. 5. The potatoes should be coated but remain chunky after a few pulses of the processor. 6. Incorporate salt and pepper according to your preference, and season with salt. 7. To serve, transfer to a bowl designed for serving, cover, and refrigerate for a few minutes.

COCONUT CURRY SAUCE

Total Time: 15 minutes | Prep Time: 10 minutes

Ingredients:

1 cup coconut milk

2 tablespoons curry powder

1 small onion, chopped

2 garlic cloves

1 tablespoon ginger, grated

Salt and pepper to taste

Directions:

1. The onion, garlic, and ginger should be combined in a food processor, and then the machine should be pulsed until the ingredients are finely chopped. 2. While the pan is heating up, add a small amount of oil and sauté the onion mixture until it develops an aromatic quality. 3. Cook for approximately one minute after adding the curry powder. 4. Blend in the coconut milk after adding it. 5. After adding salt and pepper, continue to boil for another five minutes. 6. Move the sauce back into the food processor and pulse

it until it is completely smooth. 7. You may use it as a dipping sauce or serve it warm over rice or veggies.

VEGAN PARMESAN CHEESE

Total Time: 5 minutes | Prep Time: 5 minutes

Ingredients:

½ cup raw cashews

2 tablespoons nutritional yeast

½ teaspoon garlic powder

½ teaspoon salt

Directions:

1. The cashews, nutritional yeast, garlic powder, and salt should all be placed in the food processor machine. 2. Pulse the ingredients together until they have the consistency of a fine crumb. 3. You should taste it and add additional salt if you feel it needs it. 4. Put the mixture into a jar that has a lid. 5. If you are looking for an alternative to Parmesan, sprinkle it over pasta, salads, or any other food. 6. It is possible to keep it in an airtight container for up to two weeks. 7. Before each usage, give it a good shake to ensure that it remains fresh.

MUSHROOM HERB SAUCE

Total Time: 20 minutes | Prep Time: 10 minutes

Ingredients:

1 cup mushrooms, sliced

1 shallot, chopped

1 garlic clove

½ cup vegetable broth

¼ cup coconut cream

1 tablespoon fresh thyme leaves

Salt and pepper to taste

Directions:

1. Garlic, shallot, and mushrooms should be added to the food processor immediately. Pulse until extremely finely minced. 2. Sauté mushrooms in a pan over medium heat until

softened. 3. Stir in the thyme and vegetable broth, then let it boil for five minutes. 4. Coat the sauce with coconut cream and continue to heat it until it becomes thick. 5. Move the sauce back into the food processor and pulse it until it is completely smooth. 6. Salt and pepper should be used to taste, and salt should be used to season. 7. It can be served on top of veggies, potatoes, or pasta.

PINEAPPLE SALSA

Total Time: 15 minutes | Prep Time: 10 minutes

Ingredients:

1 cup fresh pineapple chunks	1 small red onion, quartered
1 jalapeño, seeded	1 red bell pepper, cored and quartered
1/4 cup fresh cilantro leaves	Juice of 1 lime
Salt to taste	

Directions:

1. Quickly pulse the pineapple chunks in the food processor's bowl until they are coarsely diced. 2. Add the red bell pepper, jalapeño, and red onion to the mixture. Put everything through a pulse until it is coarsely chopped but still has some chunks. 3. When you have finished pulsing, add the cilantro and mix it in. 4. After pouring in the lime juice, season it to taste with salt. 5. After pulsing the ingredients together once or twice, transfer the salsa to a bowl. 6. Try it out, make any necessary adjustments to the seasoning, and serve it right away. 7. You may enjoy it with tortilla chips or as a topping for fish or meats that have been grilled.

CRANBERRY PISTACHIO BALLS

Total Time: 15 minutes + chilling time | Prep Time: 10 minutes

Ingredients:

1 cup dried cranberries	1 cup shelled pistachios
1/2 cup shredded coconut	1/4 cup honey
1/2 teaspoon vanilla extract	

Directions:

1. Put the pistachios and cranberries into the food processor and mix them together. Pulse until extremely finely minced. 2. Additionally, include honey, shredded coconut, and vanilla essence in the mixture. Pulse until everything is well blended. 3. Prepare the mixture by scooping it out with a tablespoon, and then, using your hands, roll it into balls. 4. On a dish that has been lined with parchment paper, arrange the balls evenly. 5. Put in the refrigerator for at least one hour to thicken. 6. To serve or to store, remove the dish from the refrigerator and place it in a container that is airtight. 7. As a fast snack or a nutritious dessert, you may enjoy it!

CHOCOLATE RASPBERRY BITES

Total Time: 20 minutes | Prep Time: 10 minutes

Ingredients:

1 cup dark chocolate chips	1/2 cup fresh raspberries
1/2 cup almond flour	1/4 cup unsweetened shredded coconut
1 tablespoon honey or maple syrup	

Directions:

1. To get a smooth consistency, melt the chocolate chips in a bowl that is suitable for use in the microwave for twenty seconds at a time. 2. Raspberries, almond flour, shredded coconut, and honey should be mixed together in a food processor. 3. Use a pulser to create a mixture that is thick and sticky. 4. A teaspoon's worth of the raspberry mixture should be scooped out and then rolled into balls. 5. Ensure that each ball is completely covered in chocolate by dipping it into the melted chocolate. 6. At least one hour should be spent in the refrigerator after placing

the coated bits on a dish lined with parchment paper. 7. Enjoy this delectable delicacy while it is cooled!

SMOKY CHIPOTLE SALSA

Total Time: 15 minutes | Prep Time: 10 minutes

Ingredients:

- 2 large tomatoes, quartered
- 1 chipotle pepper in adobo sauce
- 1 small onion, quartered
- 1 garlic clove
- Juice of 1 lime
- Salt and pepper to taste
- Fresh cilantro leaves for garnish (optional)

Directions:

1. Mix tomatoes, chipotle pepper, onion, and garlic in a food processor. 2. Put the ingredients through a pulse until they are roughly chopped. 3. To taste, add salt, pepper, and lime juice to the mixture. 4. While blending, maintain the texture somewhat chunky by pulsing the ingredients once or twice. 5. Put the salsa in a bowl that is suitable for serving. 6. If preferred, garnish with fresh cilantro while serving. 7. With tortilla chips, it makes a delicious topping for tacos or grilled foods.

CINNAMON RAISIN NUT BARS

Total Time: 30 minutes + chilling time | Prep Time: 15 minutes

Ingredients:

- 1 cup rolled oats
- 1 cup raw almonds
- 1/2 cup raisins
- 1/4 cup honey or maple syrup
- 1/2 teaspoon cinnamon
- 1/4 teaspoon salt

Directions:

1. Finely chop the oats and almonds by pulsing them in a food processor. 2. Add honey, cinnamon, raisins, and salt to the mixture. The mixture should be processed until it turns sticky. 3. In a pan measuring 8 inches by 8 inches and lined with parchment paper, press the ingredients out firmly. 4. Place the pan in the refrigerator for one to two hours or until the mixture has reached the desired consistency. 5. After removing from the pan, cut the mixture into bars. 6. Ensure that the container is sealed and place it in the refrigerator. 7. You can satisfy your hunger with these wholesome bars in a hurry.

VANILLA ALMOND ENERGY BARS

Total Time: 20 minutes | Prep Time: 10 minutes

Ingredients:

- 1 cup raw almonds
- 1 cup rolled oats
- ½ cup almond butter
- ¼ cup honey
- 1 teaspoon vanilla extract
- ¼ cup unsweetened coconut flakes
- Pinch of salt

Directions:

1. The almonds and oats should be pulsed in the Cuisinart food processor until they are almost completely chopped. 2. Honey, almond butter, vanilla essence, coconut flakes, and salt should be added to the mixture. 3. Prepare the mixture by processing it until it begins to come together and becomes somewhat sticky. 4. After lining a baking dish, press the mixture into it evenly. 5. After allowing it to set up in the refrigerator for half an hour, cut it into bars.

VANILLA ESPRESSO BARS

Total Time: 20 minutes | Prep Time: 10 minutes

Ingredients:

- 1 cup cashews
- 1 cup dates, pitted
- 1 tablespoon espresso powder
- 1 teaspoon vanilla extract

½ cup dark chocolate chips

1 tablespoon coconut oil (optional for smoother texture)

Directions:

1. The cashews should be pulsed in the food processor until they are finely crushed. 2. Incorporate the dates, espresso powder, and vanilla essence into the mixture and combine it until it becomes cohesive. 3. Make a smooth mixture by melting chocolate chips and coconut oil in a microwave-safe bowl. 4. Combine the chocolate mixture by adding it to the machine and pulsing it well. 5. Refrigerate the mixture for half an hour after pressing it into a dish that has been lined. 6. After cutting into bars, place them in a container that is airtight.

HONEY NUT BALLS

Total Time: 15 minutes | Prep Time: 10 minutes

Ingredients:

1 cup mixed nuts (almonds, walnuts, cashews)	1 cup dates, pitted
2 tablespoons honey	½ teaspoon cinnamon
¼ cup shredded coconut	

Directions:

1. The nuts should be pulsed in the food processor until they are roughly chopped. 2. Dates, honey, and cinnamon should be added, and the mixture should be processed until it forms a sticky dough. 3. The mixture should be scooped into tiny amounts and then rolled into balls. 4. Each ball should be coated by rolling it in crushed coconut. 5. Ten to fifteen minutes before serving, place the dish in the refrigerator to chill.

LEMON COCONUT BITES

Total Time: 15 minutes | Prep Time: 10 minutes

Ingredients:

1 cup cashews	1 cup shredded coconut
Zest of 1 lemon	2 tablespoons lemon juice
1 tablespoon maple syrup	Pinch of salt

Directions:

1. A finely chopped mixture of cashews and shredded coconut should be produced by blending them in a food processor. 2. Blend the ingredients until they come together, then add the lemon zest, lemon juice, maple syrup, and salt. 3. Make little balls out of the mixture after scooping it out. 4. In the event that you so wish, roll each ball in additional shredded coconut. 5. Before serving, let the dish chill in the refrigerator for ten minutes.

BLUEBERRY BLISS BALLS

Total Time: 20 minutes | Prep Time: 10 minutes

Ingredients:

1 cup dried blueberries	1 cup rolled oats
½ cup cashews	Two tablespoons of almond butter
1 tablespoon honey	1 teaspoon vanilla extract

Directions:

1. After the cashews, oats, and dried blueberries have been combined in the food processor, the mixture should be processed until the ingredients are roughly pulverized. 2. Almond butter, honey, and vanilla essence create a sticky dough and then process it until it reaches the desired consistency. 3. To form balls, it is necessary to scoop out little portions and then wrap them up. 4. The balls should be placed in the refrigerator for fifteen minutes in order to make them more firm. 5. You have the option of

serving it immediately or storing it in a container that is secure against air loss.

PISTACHIO CRANBERRY BARS

Total Time: 1 hour 10 minutes | Prep Time: 20 minutes

Ingredients:

1 cup shelled pistachios	1 cup dried cranberries
1 cup rolled oats	1/2 cup almond butter
1/4 cup honey	1/4 teaspoon salt
1/2 teaspoon vanilla extract	

Directions:

1. Bake for a few minutes at 325°F (160°C) on high. Using parchment paper, line a baking pan that is 8 inches by 8 inches. 2. The food processor should be used to combine the oats and pistachios. To roughly chop, pulse the ingredients. 3. Add honey, almond butter, cranberries, salt, and vanilla extract to the mixture. Process the ingredients until they start to clump together. 4. Spread the ingredients out evenly in the prepared baking pan. 5. The edges should be golden brown after 25 to 30 minutes in the oven. Allow the pan to cool down. 6. The bars can be taken out of the pan by lifting the parchment paper. 7. Cut into squares, and either serve immediately or keep in a container that is airtight.

SALTED CARAMEL BITES

Total Time: 50 minutes | Prep Time: 15 minutes

Ingredients:

1 cup dates, pitted	1/2 cup almond flour
1/4 teaspoon sea salt	1/4 cup coconut oil, melted
1 teaspoon vanilla extract	1/4 cup dark chocolate chips (optional)

Directions:

1. Dates, almond flour, natural sea salt, and coconut oil should all be placed in the food processor. 2. When necessary, scrape down the sides of the bowl as you process the mixture until it is smooth and sticky. 3. To blend, add the vanilla extract and pulse the mixture. 4. Roll the mixture into little balls using a tablespoon as a scooping measuring device. 5. The nibbles can be topped with melted chocolate or dipped halfway, depending on your preference. 6. Refrigerate the bits for half an hour or until they have reached the desired consistency. 7. Ensure that the container is sealed and place it in the refrigerator.

MOCHA PECAN BALLS

Total Time: 1 hour | Prep Time: 20 minutes

Ingredients:

1 cup pecans	1 cup rolled oats
1/4 cup cocoa powder	1 tablespoon instant espresso powder
1/4 cup maple syrup	1/4 teaspoon salt
1/2 teaspoon vanilla extract	

Directions:

1. The food processor should be stocked with oats and pecans. Blend until the mixture is very fine. 2. Cocoa powder, espresso powder, salt, and vanilla extract should be added. To blend, give it a quick pulse. 3. Maple syrup should be drizzled in as the ingredients are being processed until it forms a dough. 4. Pinch the dough between your hands and roll it into 1-inch balls. 5. Place balls on a dish lined with parchment paper and place in the refrigerator for half an hour. 6. In order to give a final touch, you can roll the balls in more cocoa powder if you so choose. 7. Ensure that the container is sealed and place it in the refrigerator.

SPICY CILANTRO DIP

Total Time: 10 minutes | Prep Time: 5 minutes

Ingredients:

1 cup fresh cilantro, packed	1/2 cup Greek yogurt
1 clove garlic, minced	1 tablespoon lime juice
1/2 jalapeño, seeded	Salt and pepper to taste

Directions:

1. Chopped cilantro, Greek yogurt, garlic, and lime juice should all be placed in the food processor. 2. Jalapeño, salt, and pepper should be added. Pulse until everything is well blended and smooth. 3. Try it out and make any necessary adjustments to the salt, pepper, or lime juice. 4. If you want to chill the dip for a few minutes, transfer it to a bowl and set it aside. 5. Spread it on bread, serve it with chips, or use it as a spread. 6. Seal any remaining food in an airtight container and store it in the fridge. 7. Take pleasure in the flavor within two to three days.

PUMPKIN SPICE BARS

Total Time: 45 minutes | Prep Time: 10 minutes

Ingredients:

1 cup canned pumpkin puree	1 cup all-purpose flour
1/2 cup brown sugar	1/2 cup granulated sugar
1/2 cup vegetable oil	2 large eggs
1 tsp vanilla extract	1 tsp baking powder
1/2 tsp baking soda	1/2 tsp salt
1 1/2 tsp pumpkin pie spice	

Directions:

1. Set the oven to 350°F (175°C) and put parchment paper in a baking pan. 2. In the food processor, combine pumpkin puree, sugars, oil, eggs, and vanilla; process until smooth. 3. Toss in the flour, baking soda, pumpkin pie spice, baking powder, and pulse until just combined. 4. When the baking pan is ready, pour in the batter and level it out. 5. Bake for twenty-five to thirty minutes or until a toothpick inserted in the center of the cake extracts clean. 6. After allowing the pan to cool for ten minutes, move the pan to a wire rack to finish cooling entirely. 7. Cut into bars and serve.

CREAMY RANCH DRESSING

Total Time: 10 minutes | Prep Time: 10 minutes

Ingredients:

1/2 cup mayonnaise	1/2 cup sour cream
1/4 cup buttermilk (or more for a thinner consistency)	1 clove garlic, minced
2 tbsp fresh parsley, chopped	1 tbsp fresh dill, chopped
1 tbsp fresh chives, chopped	1/2 tsp onion powder
1/2 tsp salt	1/4 tsp black pepper

Directions:

1. Add buttermilk, sour cream, and mayonnaise to the food processor and pulse until smooth. 2. Garlic, parsley, dill, chives, onion powder, freshly ground black pepper, and salt should be added. 3. Mix until it is completely smooth and well-blended. 4. Take a taste, and make any necessary adjustments to the seasoning. 5. Adjust the amount of buttermilk by adding a spoonful at a time if you want the dressing to be thinner. 6. Put the mixture into a jar or other container, cover it, and place it in the refrigerator for at least half an hour to allow the flavors to combine. 7. Serve as a dip, with salads, or with vegetables.

PUMPKIN PECAN BARS

Total Time: 50 minutes | Prep Time: 15 minutes

Ingredients:

1 cup canned pumpkin puree	1/2 cup all-purpose flour

1/2 cup oats	1/4 cup brown sugar
1/4 cup maple syrup	1/4 cup melted butter
1/2 cup pecans, chopped	1/2 tsp cinnamon
1/4 tsp nutmeg	1/4 tsp salt

Directions:

1. Set a parchment-lined baking sheet in a preheated oven set to 175 degrees Celsius (350 degrees Fahrenheit). 2. Blend together the flour, oats, brown sugar, cinnamon, nutmeg, and salt in the food processor. Pulse the mixture to blend the ingredients. 3. To make a soft dough, add pumpkin puree, maple syrup, and melted butter, and then pulse the ingredients until they meet. 4. The dough should be spread out evenly in the baking pan, and then pecans should be sprinkled on top. 5. The nuts should be gently pressed into the dough with a spatula. 6. Bake the cake for thirty to thirty-five minutes or until the edges are golden brown. 7. Wait until the bars have totally cooled before serving.

CHOCOLATE PISTACHIO BARS

Total Time: 40 minutes | Prep Time: 15 minutes

Ingredients:

1 cup all-purpose flour	1/2 cup sugar
1/2 cup unsalted butter, melted	1/2 cup chopped pistachios
1/2 cup chocolate chips	1 large egg
1 tsp vanilla extract	1/4 tsp salt

Directions:

1. Spray a baking pan with butter and set the oven temperature to 350°F. 2. Add flour, sugar, butter, and salt to a food processor and pulse until crumbly. 3. The mixture should be pulsed until it begins to come together after the addition of the egg and the vanilla essence. 4. Through the use of a spatula, incorporate the chocolate chips and pistachios. 5. Create a uniform layer of the mixture that has been prepared in the baking pan. 6. Bake for twenty to twenty-five minutes or until the top is just beginning to turn brown. 7. Remove from the heat, cut into bars, and serve.

BEETROOT HUMMUS

Total Time: 15 minutes | Prep Time: 10 minutes

Ingredients:

1 medium beet, cooked and peeled	1 can (15 oz) chickpeas
1/4 cup tahini	2 tbsp lemon juice
1 clove garlic, minced	1/4 tsp ground cumin
Salt to taste	2–3 tbsp olive oil

Directions:

1. The beets, chickpeas, tahini, lemon juice, garlic, and cumin should all be placed in the food processor once they have been cooked. 2. Make sure the mixture is totally smooth by scraping down the bowl's edges as needed. 3. While continuing to process, keep adding olive oil in increments until the desired consistency is achieved. 4. After a quick mixing process, season with salt according to your preference. 5. The seasonings should be tasted and adjusted, with additional lemon juice or garlic being added as required. 6. Transfer to a bowl that may be used for serving, and if preferred, sprinkle with more vegetable oil. 7. Served as a spread, with pita bread, or with vegetables.

CARAMEL CASHEW BARS

Total Time: 40 minutes | Prep Time: 15 minutes

Ingredients:

1 cup flour	½ cup brown sugar, packed
½ cup unsalted butter, softened	½ cup sweetened condensed milk
1 cup caramel bits	1 cup cashews, chopped

1 tsp vanilla extract | ½ cup semisweet chocolate chips (optional for topping)

Directions:

1. The oven should be set on high heat (350 degrees Fahrenheit, 175 degrees Celsius). 2. Use parchment paper to line an 8-by-8-inch baking dish. 3. Process flour, brown sugar, and butter in a food processor to make a crumbly mixture. Once the dish is ready, press the mixture into it. 4. After 10 to 12 minutes in the oven, the crust should be brown. Take it out of the oven and put it aside. 5. The caramel pieces and sweetened condensed milk should be heated together in a saucepan over low heat until completely smooth. Cashews and vanilla should be stirred in. 6. After you've distributed the crust evenly, pour the caramel mixture on top. If you'd like, you may top it with chocolate chips. 7. Continue baking for another 12–15 minutes or until the caramel has hardened. Let it cool entirely before slicing it into bars.

MAPLE ALMOND BALLS

Total Time: 25 minutes | Prep Time: 10 minutes

Ingredients:

1 cup almonds	1 cup rolled oats
½ cup maple syrup	1 tsp vanilla extract
¼ tsp sea salt	1 cup shredded coconut for rolling

Directions:

1. The almonds should be crushed to a very fine consistency using a food processor, which should be used to pulse them. Combine the oats by pulsing them once more after adding them. 2. The mixture should be processed until it is able to stay together after adding the maple syrup, vanilla, and sea salt. 3. Form the mixture into balls measuring one inch in diameter using your hands. 4. Each ball should be covered with crushed coconut before being rolled. 5. Position on a baking sheet that has been covered with

parchment paper. Ten to fifteen minutes before serving, place in the refrigerator.

CURRIED CARROT SOUP

Total Time: 35 minutes | Prep Time: 10 minutes

Ingredients:

1 tbsp olive oil	1 small onion, chopped
1 lb carrots, peeled and chopped	2 cups vegetable broth
1 tsp curry powder	½ cup coconut milk
Salt and pepper, to taste	

Directions:

1. To prepare the olive oil, heat it in a big saucepan until it reaches a temperature of medium. Sauté the onion until it has attained a mellow state. 2. Cook the carrots for a further five minutes after adding them. 3. Boil the veggie broth after adding it. Lower the heat, cover, and boil the carrots for 15 minutes until tender. 4. After adding curry powder, blend the mixture in a food processor until smooth. 5. Put the mixture back into the pot, whisk in the coconut milk, and season it with garlic powder and salt. Please bring to a boil before serving.

MANGO CHUTNEY

Total Time: 45 minutes | Prep Time: 10 minutes

Ingredients:

2 ripe mangoes, peeled and chopped	½ cup apple cider vinegar
½ cup sugar	1 small onion, chopped
1 garlic clove, minced	1 tsp grated ginger
¼ tsp red pepper flakes	Salt, to taste

Directions:

1. Mangoes, vinegar, sugar, onion, garlic, and ginger should be mixed together in a saucepan as

stated above. 2. Turn the heat down to medium-low and simmer for a while after it boils. 3. For around half an hour, stir the mixture on periodically until it begins to thicken. 4. Flakes of red pepper and salt should be added to taste. 5. Prior to serving, allow to cool. Ensure that the container is airtight and store it in the refrigerator.

FRESH HERB SALSA

Total Time: 15 minutes | Prep Time: 10 minutes

Ingredients:

1 cup fresh cilantro leaves	1 cup fresh parsley leaves
1 small tomato, chopped	1 small onion, chopped
1 garlic clove, minced	1 tbsp lime juice
Salt and pepper, to taste	

Directions:

1. To finely chop the cilantro and parsley, place them in the food processor and pulse until they are smooth. 2. To combine the tomato, onion, and garlic, just give the food processor a few pulses. 3. The salsa should be pulsed until it achieves the required consistency, after which lime juice, salt, and pepper should be added. 4. Transfer to a bowl, and make any necessary adjustments to the seasoning. 5. Eat it fresh with chips or use it as a topping for meats that have been grilled.

CHOCOLATE ALMOND FUDGE BARS

Total Time: 2 hours (includes chilling) | Prep Time: 15 minutes

Ingredients:

1 cup almonds	1 cup dates, pitted
1/2 cup cocoa powder	1/4 cup coconut oil, melted
1/4 tsp sea salt	1 tsp vanilla extract

Directions:

1. After adding the almonds to the food processor, pulse them until they are completely ground. 2. Dates, cocoa powder, vanilla essence, and powdered sea salt should be added. 3. The ingredients should be blended until they form a sticky dough. Blend in the melted coconut oil until it is completely incorporated. 4. Put the mixture into a baking dish that has been lined with parchment paper. 5. Place in the refrigerator for one to two hours or until the mixture becomes solid. 6. In order to serve, cut into squares. 7. Place in an airtight jar and place in the refrigerator.

SUNDRIED TOMATO PESTO

Total Time: 10 minutes | Prep Time: 5 minutes

Ingredients:

1/2 cup sun-dried tomatoes	1/4 cup fresh basil leaves
1/4 cup grated Parmesan cheese	1/4 cup pine nuts or walnuts
1 clove garlic	1/3 cup olive oil

Directions:

1. Sun-dried tomatoes, basil, Parmesan cheese, almonds, and garlic should all be placed in the food processor. 2. Proceed to pulse the items until they are roughly chopped. 3. Slowly add olive oil to the pesto while the machine is operating until the pesto is completely smooth. 4. Whenever necessary, scrape down the sides and then combine once more. 5. If you like, you may adjust the seasoning by adding salt and pepper. 6. Create a spread or use it as a topping for spaghetti. 7. Place it in an airtight jar and place it in the refrigerator for up to a week.

SWEET ONION RELISH

Total Time: 30 minutes | Prep Time: 10 minutes

Ingredients:

2 large sweet onions, chopped	1/2 cup apple cider vinegar

1/4 cup brown sugar   1/4 tsp salt

1/4 tsp black pepper

Directions:

1. Insert the onions into the food processor and pulse them until they are chopped very finely. 2. In a saucepan, mix vinegar, brown sugar, salt, and pepper with onions. 3. After boiling, reduce the heat to simmer. 4. Cook for fifteen to twenty minutes, stirring the mixture regularly, until the relish thickens and the onions become tender. 5. Take the pan off the heat and let it cool. 6. Place the mixture in a jar and place it in the refrigerator until you are ready to use it. 7. You may use it as a topping on sandwiches, meats, or cheeses for serving.

BLACK OLIVE TAPENADE

Total Time: 10 minutes | Prep Time: 5 minutes

Ingredients:

1 cup black olives, pitted	1 tbsp capers, rinsed
1 clove garlic	1/4 cup fresh parsley
1/4 cup olive oil	1 tsp lemon juice

Directions:

1. Put the olives, capers, garlic, and parsley into the food processor and proceed to process. 2. Pulse until the mixture is coarsely minced. 3. After adding the lemon juice and olive oil, combine the mixture until it smoothes out. 4. If you feel it's necessary, adjust the salt and pepper to taste. 5. The tapenade should be transferred to a dish for serving. 6. As a condiment, serve with crackers or toast, or use it alone. 7. You may keep it in the refrigerator for up to a week if you store it in an airtight container.

CLASSIC HUMMUS DIP

Total Time: 10 minutes | Prep Time: 5 minutes

Ingredients:

1 can (15 oz) chickpeas	1/4 cup tahini

2 tbsp lemon juice   1 clove garlic

1/4 cup olive oil   Salt and pepper, to taste

Directions:

1. To the food processor, add garlic, chickpeas, tahini, and lemon juice. Proceed to process. 2. Add a few tablespoons of water to get the appropriate consistency, and mix until smooth. 3. While the machine is running, gradually add olive oil until the mixture becomes creamy. 4. After scraping down the sides, mix the ingredients together until they are completely incorporated. 5. In addition to seasoning with salt, add pepper and salt to taste. The hummus should be placed in a serving bowl, and if desired, olive oil could be drizzled over it. 6. You may serve it as a spread, with pita, or with veggies.

CREAMY TOMATO SOUP

Total Time: 30 minutes | Prep Time: 10 minutes

Ingredients:

2 tablespoons olive oil	1 medium onion, chopped
2 cloves garlic, minced	1 can (28 ounces) crushed tomatoes
2 cups vegetable broth	1 teaspoon sugar
1 teaspoon dried basil	Salt and pepper to taste
½ cup heavy cream	Fresh basil for garnish (optional)

Directions:

1. Mince the garlic and onion in a Cuisinart food processor. 2. A big saucepan filled with olive oil should be heated over medium heat. Saute the garlic and onion for approximately 5 minutes or until they are tender. 3. Toss in some smashed tomatoes, veggie stock, sugar, dried basil, pepper, and salt. After reaching a boil, return to a simmer for fifteen minutes. 4. Put the soup in batches and carefully transfer each batch to the food processor. Blend until it is completely

smooth. 5. Return the soup that has been pureed to the pot, then pour in the heavy cream and bring the mixture to a boil. 6. Reevaluate the seasoning by tasting. 7. Whether you prefer it hot or cold, top with fresh basil and serve.

MAPLE TAHINI DRESSING

Total Time: 10 minutes | Prep Time: 5 minutes

Ingredients:

¼ cup tahini	3 tablespoons maple syrup
2 tablespoons apple cider vinegar	1 tablespoon soy sauce
1 clove garlic, minced	¼ cup water (adjust for desired consistency)
Salt and pepper to taste	

Directions:

1. Put the tahini, maple syrup, apple cider vinegar, soy sauce, and minced garlic into your Cuisinart Food Processor and mix them together before proceeding. 2. Pulse until everything is completely combined and smooth. 3. Gradually include water into the mixture until you get the required consistency. 4. The dressing should be tasted, and salt and pepper should be added as necessary. 5. If the consistency is too thick, stir in a little bit more water and combine once more. 6. Remove the dressing from the dish and place it in a jar. 7. Put in the refrigerator until you are ready to use it; mix it to serve.

MOCHA ALMOND BALLS

Total Time: 20 minutes | Prep Time: 10 minutes

Ingredients:

1 cup almonds	1 cup Medjool dates, pitted
2 tablespoons cocoa powder	1 tablespoon instant coffee granules
1 teaspoon vanilla extract	A pinch of salt
Unsweetened shredded coconut (optional for coating)	

Directions:

1. Put the almonds in your Cuisinart Food Processor and pulse them until they are completely ground. 2. Include the dates that have been pitted, cocoa powder, instant coffee, vanilla essence, and salt in the mixture. Blend until a sticky dough is formed. 3. Assemble the ingredients into little balls with a diameter of approximately one inch. 4. In order to coat the balls, you might choose to roll them in shredded coconut. 5. On a parchment-lined baking sheet, place almond balls in a single layer. 6. Allow to chill in the refrigerator for at least ten minutes to set. 7. Here it is, ready to be enjoyed as a dessert or snack!

SPICY MANGO SALSA

Total Time: 15 minutes | Prep Time: 10 minutes

Ingredients:

2 ripe mangoes, peeled and diced	1 small red onion, chopped
1 red bell pepper, diced	1 jalapeño, seeded and chopped
Juice of 1 lime	¼ cup fresh cilantro, chopped
Salt to taste	

Directions:

1. Chop the onion, dice the mango, and add the red bell pepper and jalapeño to your Cuisinart Food Processor. 2. Process in a food processor until the ingredients are minced but not pureed. 3. Mix in the salt, cilantro, and lime juice after transferring to a bowl. 4. Adjust the seasoning according to your taste. 5. After 10 minutes, the salsa's flavors will have melded. 6. As a topping for grilled meats or to go with tortilla chips,

serve. 7. Any excess can be refrigerated for a maximum of two days.

CHILI LIME DIP

Total Time: 10 minutes | Prep Time: 5 minutes

Ingredients:

1 cup sour cream	2 tablespoons mayonnaise
Juice of 1 lime	1 teaspoon chili powder
½ teaspoon garlic powder	Salt to taste

Directions:

1. Mix mayonnaise, sour cream, lime juice, chili powder, garlic powder, and salt in a Cuisinart food processor. 2. Mix until blended and completely smooth. 3. If you want it spicier, add additional chili powder or lime juice to taste. 4. Place a serving dish over the dip. 5. To get the most out of the flavors, let it chill in the fridge for 10 minutes before you serve. 6. As a spread, with tortilla chips, or alongside veggies. 7. Put any remaining food in a sealed container and refrigerate for no more than three days.

BERRY COCONUT BARS

Total Time: 40 minutes | Prep Time: 15 minutes

Ingredients:

1 cup rolled oats	1 cup unsweetened shredded coconut
1/2 cup almond flour	1/2 cup honey or maple syrup
1/2 cup mixed berries	1/4 cup coconut oil, melted
1 tsp vanilla extract	1/2 tsp salt

Directions:

1. Set an 8x8-inch baking pan with parchment paper in a 350°F (175°C) oven. 2. Toss together the rolled oats, almond flour, shredded coconut, honey (or maple syrup), melted coconut oil, vanilla extract, and salt in a Cuisinart food processor. Mix by pulsing. 3. Pulse a few times to integrate the mixed berries; be careful not to overmix. 4. After getting the baking pan ready, pour in the mixture and use a spatula to push it down evenly. 5. To get a beautiful brown crust, bake for 25 minutes. Take it out of the oven and set it aside to cool in the pan. 6. Cut into bars and serve after chilled.

MINT CHOCOLATE BARS

Total Time: 1 hour | Prep Time: 20 minutes

Ingredients:

1 cup almond flour	1/2 cup cocoa powder
1/4 cup coconut oil, melted	1/4 cup maple syrup
1/4 cup fresh mint leaves	1/4 cup dark chocolate chips
1/2 tsp peppermint extract	Pinch of salt

Directions:

1. Toss some salt, cocoa powder, almond flour, maple syrup, and warmed coconut oil into your Cuisinart food processor. 2. Mix until a ball is formed. 3. Blend in the peppermint oil and fresh mint leaves by pulsing until the mint is finely minced. 4. Use parchment paper to line the bottom of a small square baking dish. Press the mixture into the dish evenly. 5. Once the pressed mixture is properly coated, add melted dark chocolate chips on top. You may use a microwave or double boiler to melt the chips. 6. After 40 minutes, or until the dish is solid, transfer it to the fridge. 7. After it sets, cut it into bars and enjoy them cold.

RASPBERRY LEMON BALLS

Total Time: 30 minutes | Prep Time: 15 minutes

Ingredients:

1 cup dates, pitted	1/2 cup raw almonds

1/2 cup freeze-dried raspberries

Zest of 1 lemon

Juice of 1 lemon

1/4 cup unsweetened shredded coconut

Pinch of salt

Directions:

1. Blend the dates that have been pitted and the raw almonds in your Cuisinart Food Processor until the mixture is finely minced. 2. Raspberry freeze-dried, lemon zest, lemon juice, shredded coconut, and salt should be added to the mixture. The mixture should be thoroughly mixed and sticky. 3. Applying pressure with your hands, shape the mixture into little balls with a diameter of approximately one inch. 4. Line a tray with parchment paper and place the balls on it. 5. Put the mixture into the refrigerator for fifteen minutes so that it will become more solid. 6. It can be served either cold or at room temperature.

LEMON PEPPER BUTTER

Total Time: 10 minutes | Prep Time: 10 minutes

Ingredients:

1 cup unsalted butter, softened

Zest of 1 lemon

1 tbsp fresh lemon juice

1 tsp black pepper

1/2 tsp sea salt

Directions:

1. A mixture of butter that has been softened, lemon zest, lemon juice, black pepper, and sea salt should be added to your Cuisinart Food Processor. 2. Till the mixture is perfectly smooth and fully combined, keep processing. 3. Reprocess the mixture after scraping down the edges to verify that it is evenly mixed. 4. Spoon the butter with lemon pepper onto a sheet of parchment paper or plastic wrap. 5. Mold into the shape of a log, and then twist the ends together to seal. Until it becomes hard, chill in the refrigerator. 6. By the time you are ready to serve, cut into rounds.

ZESTY CORN SALSA

Total Time: 15 minutes | Prep Time: 15 minutes

Ingredients:

2 cups fresh corn kernels (or canned/frozen corn)

1/2 red onion, chopped

1 bell pepper, diced

1 jalapeño, seeded and chopped

1/4 cup fresh cilantro, chopped

Juice of 1 lime

Salt and pepper to taste

Directions:

1. Using your Cuisinart Food Processor, blend corn kernels, red onion, bell pepper, jalapeño, and cilantro according to your preference. A few pulses will chop everything up into a coarser consistency. 2. While pulsing once more, add the lime juice, salt, and pepper to the mixture. 3. Take a taste, and make any necessary adjustments to the seasoning. 4. After transferring the mixture to a serving bowl, allow it to sit for ten minutes so that the flavors may combine. 5. Serve as a topping for tacos or with tortilla chips, either refrigerated or at room temperature at your discretion.

WHITE BEAN DIP

Total Time: 10 minutes | Prep Time: 10 minutes

Ingredients:

1 can (15 oz) white beans, drained and rinsed

2 tablespoons tahini

2 tablespoons lemon juice

1 clove garlic, minced

2 tablespoons olive oil

Salt and pepper to taste

Fresh parsley for garnish (optional)

Directions:

1. Put the white beans, tahini, lemon juice, and garlic that have been minced into your Cuisinart Food Processor and bring them together. 2. Pulse the ingredients together until they are completely smooth and creamy. 3. While the food processor is operating, the olive oil should be drizzled in until it is completely integrated. 4. Taste and adjust salt and pepper; mix for a few seconds to thoroughly integrate the elements. Transfer to a bowl that may be used for serving, and if wanted, sprinkle with a small bit of olive oil. 5. Immediately prior to serving, garnish with fresh parsley. 6. Pita chips or fresh vegetables can be served alongside.

VANILLA ALMOND BITES

Total Time: 15 minutes | Prep Time: 15 minutes

Ingredients:

1 cup raw almonds	1 cup pitted dates
1 teaspoon vanilla extract	1/4 teaspoon salt
1/2 cup shredded coconut (optional)	

Directions:

1. Prepare the almonds by pulsing them in the Cuisinart Food Processor until they are coarsely ground. 2. Add the dates that have been pitted, vanilla essence, and salt, and pulse until a dough that is sticky is formed. 3. If preferred, grated coconut can be used in the recipe to provide another texture. 4. Form the mixture into balls by scooping out sections of it that are about the size of a tablespoon. 5. Placing the bits on a baking sheet that has been lined with parchment? 6. In order to firm up, place the mixture in the refrigerator for approximately half an hour. 7. For a quick snack or a surge of energy, enjoy!

MOCHA ALMOND ENERGY BITES

Total Time: 15 minutes | Prep Time: 15 minutes

Ingredients:

1 cup raw almonds	1 cup pitted dates
2 tablespoons cocoa powder	1 tablespoon instant coffee granules
1/4 teaspoon salt	1/4 cup chocolate chips (optional)

Directions:

1. Prepare the almonds by pulsing them in the Cuisinart Food Processor until they are coarsely ground. 2. Blend the dates that have been pitted, cocoa powder, coffee granules, and salt until they are completely blended. 3. If using, add the chocolate chips and whisk them in until they are distributed uniformly. 4. Use your hands to shape the mixture into little pieces. 5. Line a tray with parchment paper and place the energy bites on it. 6. For the best results, refrigerate for at least half an hour. 7. Place it in an airtight jar and place it in the refrigerator for up to a week.

WALNUT FUDGE BITES

Total Time: 20 minutes | Prep Time: 20 minutes

Ingredients:

1 cup walnuts	1 cup pitted dates
2 tablespoons cocoa powder	1 teaspoon vanilla extract
1/4 teaspoon salt	

Directions:

1. Prepare the walnuts by pulsing them in the Cuisinart Food Processor until they are finely ground. 2. Proceed to process the dates that have been pitted, cocoa powder, vanilla essence, and salt until they are well blended. 3. When pushed, the mixture ought to take on a sticky consistency and remain cohesive. 4. Roll the mixture into balls using tablespoon-sized portions that you scoop out. 5. Place on a baking sheet that has been lined with parchment paper. 6. Allow it to chill in the refrigerator for at least half an hour to

set. 7. Indulge in this delicious and nutritious dessert or snack!

TAHINI SAUCE

Total Time: 5 minutes | Prep Time: 5 minutes

Ingredients:

1/2 cup tahini	1/4 cup water (more as needed)
2 tablespoons lemon juice	1 clove garlic, minced
Salt to taste	

Directions:

1. Put the tahini, water, lemon juice, and garlic that has been minced into the Cuisinart Food Processor. Continue processing. 2. If you want a thinner consistency, add water and blend until smooth and creamy. 3. Add salt to taste, and process for a few seconds to incorporate the ingredients. 4. Make any necessary adjustments to the taste by adding additional garlic or lemon juice. 5. It can be served immediately or refrigerated in an airtight container. Utilize as a dressing, a dip, or a drizzle over the meals that you enjoy the most.

CREAMY DILL SAUCE

Total Time: 10 minutes | Prep Time: 10 minutes

Ingredients:

1 cup Greek yogurt	2 tablespoons fresh dill, chopped
1 tablespoon lemon juice	1 clove garlic, minced
Salt and pepper to taste	

Directions:

1. Greek yogurt, dill, lemon juice, and garlic that have been minced should be mixed together while using your Cuisinart Food Processor. 2. Blend all of the ingredients together until they are completely combined and smooth. 3. Taste, season with salt and pepper, then pulse fast to mix the components. 4. Depending on your own liking, adjust the amount of spice or dill. 5. After transferring to a serving bowl, place in the refrigerator for half an hour to let the flavors combine. 6. This can be used as a condiment, a dressing, or a dip. 7. Take pleasure in using it as a sandwich spread, with grilled meats, or with veggies.

LEMON BLUEBERRY BITES

Total Time: 30 minutes | Prep Time: 15 minutes

Ingredients:

1 cup rolled oats	1/2 cup almond flour
1/4 cup honey or maple syrup	1/4 cup coconut oil, melted
Zest of 1 lemon	1 tablespoon lemon juice
1 cup fresh blueberries	1/4 teaspoon salt

Directions:

1. Put the rolled oats, almond flour, honey, melted coconut oil, lemon zest, lemon juice, and salt into the Cuisinart food processor. Process until everything is nicely combined. Pulse until everything is well blended. 2. While using a spatula, carefully incorporate the fresh blueberries into the mixture, taking care not to smash them. 3. Put the mixture into a baking dish that has been lined with parchment paper and push it down firmly into the bottom. 4. In order to firm up, place the mixture in the refrigerator for fifteen minutes. 5. Remove from the refrigerator or serve at room temperature after being cut into little squares or bars.

HAZELNUT MOCHA BARS

Total Time: 1 hour | Prep Time: 20 minutes

Ingredients:

1 cup hazelnuts	1 cup pitted dates
1/4 cup cocoa powder	1 tablespoon instant coffee

1/4 teaspoon salt

1 tablespoon coconut oil

1/2 cup dark chocolate chips

Directions:

1. After placing the hazelnuts in the food processor, pulse them until they are finely chopped but not quite a paste. 2. Mix in some salt, cocoa powder, instant coffee, and dates that have been pitted. The mixture should be processed until it comes together. 3. Using parchment paper, line a baking dish that is 8 inches by 8 inches. 4. Using a hard pressing motion, press the mixture into the bottom of the dish. 5. Blend dark chocolate chips and coconut oil in a microwave-safe bowl until smooth. Cover the bars with a drizzle. 6. After allowing it to set in the refrigerator for half an hour, cut it into bars and serve it.

CHOCOLATE COCONUT ENERGY BITES

Total Time: 20 minutes | Prep Time: 10 minutes

Ingredients:

1 cup pitted dates	1/2 cup almond flour
1/4 cup cocoa powder	1/4 cup unsweetened shredded coconut
1 tablespoon coconut oil	1 teaspoon vanilla extract
Pinch of salt	

Directions:

1. Dates that have been pitted, almond flour, cocoa powder, shredded coconut, coconut oil, vanilla essence, and salt, should be the ingredients that are combined in the food processor. 2. Work the mixture until it forms a sticky dough. 3. Make the mixture into little balls with a diameter of around one inch by rolling it with your palms. 4. The balls can be rolled in more shredded coconut if that is what you want. 5. Divide the energy bits among themselves on a

parchment paper-lined baking sheet. 6. Before serving, place the mixture in the refrigerator for ten minutes to allow it to become more solid.

WALNUT BASIL PESTO

Total Time: 10 minutes | Prep Time: 10 minutes

Ingredients:

2 cups fresh basil leaves	1/2 cup walnuts
1/4 cup grated Parmesan cheese	2 cloves garlic
1/4 cup olive oil	Salt and pepper to taste

Directions:

1. Mix the basil leaves, walnuts, Parmesan cheese, and garlic in the food processor until everything is nicely combined. Pulse until the mixture is roughly chopped. 2. While the food processor is operating, gradually incorporate olive oil into the mixture until it is thoroughly combined. 3. Salt and pepper should be added to taste, and the mixture should be blended until it reaches the appropriate consistency. 4. The pesto should be transferred to a jar and then stored in the refrigerator for a period of up to one week. 5. This sauce may be used as a dip, over sandwiches, or over pasta.

ORANGE CREAMSICLE BITES

Total Time: 45 minutes | Prep Time: 15 minutes

Ingredients:

1 cup cashews, soaked for 2 hours	1/2 cup pitted dates
1/4 cup orange juice	Zest of 1 orange
1/4 cup shredded coconut	1 teaspoon vanilla extract
Pinch of salt	

Directions:

1. The soaked cashews should be rinsed and drained before being added to the food

processor. 2. Before adding salt, pitted dates, orange zest, shredded coconut, vanilla essence, and orange juice, stir in the ingredients. Blend or process till fluffy and velvety. 3. Firmly press the mixture into silicone molds or little muffin pans. 4. Set in the freezer for approximately half an hour. 5. Take the bits out of the molds when they are hard, and then put them in a freezer-safe container.

VEGAN NACHO CHEESE

Total Time: 15 minutes | Prep Time: 10 minutes

Ingredients:

1 cup raw cashews	1/4 cup nutritional yeast
1/4 cup water (more as needed)	1 tablespoon lemon juice
1 teaspoon garlic powder	1/2 teaspoon onion powder
1/2 teaspoon smoked paprika	1/2 teaspoon salt
1/4 teaspoon cayenne pepper (optional)	

Directions:

1. Throw the soaked cashews, nutritional yeast, water, lemon juice, garlic powder, onion powder, smoked paprika, salt, and cayenne pepper into the Cuisinart Food Processor. Make sure to mix well. 2. With occasional scraping of the sides, process until a creamy consistency is achieved. 3. To adjust the consistency to your liking, add water a tablespoon at a time if the mixture seems too thick. 4. If needed, taste and make adjustments to the seasoning. 5. Pour the cheese sauce into a dish and set aside to serve. 6. With tortilla chips and vegetables or as a topping for your favorite recipes, enjoy warm or at room temperature.

ROASTED GARLIC SPREAD

Total Time: 30 minutes | Prep Time: 10 minutes

Ingredients:

1 whole bulb of garlic	1 tablespoon olive oil
1/4 teaspoon salt	1/4 teaspoon black pepper
1/4 cup vegan cream cheese	

Directions:

1. Adjust the oven's temperature to either 200°C or 400°F. 2. To reveal the cloves, slice the top off the garlic bulb and sprinkle with olive oil. 3. Roast the bulb for 25-30 minutes, covered with aluminum foil, until it becomes tender. 4. After cooling, add the roasted garlic cloves to the Cuisinart food processor by pressing them firmly. 5. If using, sprinkle vegan cream cheese over top and season with salt and pepper. 6. Blend or process until very creamy, stopping to scrape down edges as necessary. 7. Use as a dip for vegetables, on crackers, or on crusty toast.

VEGAN CAESAR DRESSING

Total Time: 10 minutes | Prep Time: 5 minutes

Ingredients:

1/2 cup raw cashews	1/4 cup water
2 tablespoons lemon juice	1 tablespoon Dijon mustard
1 tablespoon capers, drained	1 clove garlic
1/4 teaspoon salt	1/4 teaspoon black pepper
1/4 teaspoon nutritional yeast (optional)	

Directions:

1. Juice from the lemon, Dijon mustard, capers, garlic, salt, black pepper, nutritional yeast (if used), and soaked cashews should be mixed together in the Cuisinart food processor. 2. With occasional scraping of the sides, process until a

creamy consistency is achieved. 3. Salt, lemon juice, and pepper can be adjusted to taste. 4. To adjust the dressing's thickness, add water a tablespoon at a time until it's the right consistency. 5. Pour over salads right away or refrigerate for up to a week in an airtight container.

SPICY PEANUT SAUCE

Total Time: 10 minutes | Prep Time: 5 minutes

Ingredients:

1/2 cup peanut butter	1/4 cup soy sauce or tamari
2 tablespoons maple syrup or agave nectar	2 tablespoons rice vinegar
1 tablespoon sesame oil	1 clove garlic
1 teaspoon grated ginger	1-2 teaspoons sriracha or chili paste (to taste)
Water (to thin, as needed)	

Directions:

1. Peanut butter, soy sauce, maple syrup, rice vinegar, sesame oil, garlic, ginger, and sriracha should all be mixed together in the Cuisinart Food Processor. 2. Scrape down the edges of the bowl as needed to ensure a smooth processing. 3. Stir in a tablespoon of water at a time until the sauce reaches the consistency you like, if it's too thick. 4. Add extra sriracha to taste for desired spiciness. 5. Toss with noodles, salads, or grilled veggies for a delicious dip, dressing, or sauce. 6. Keep any leftovers for up to a week in the fridge if sealed tightly.

CREAMY LEMON HERB DIP

Total Time: 10 minutes | Prep Time: 10 minutes

Ingredients:

1 cup Greek yogurt	1/2 cup sour cream
2 tablespoons fresh lemon juice	Zest of 1 lemon
1 teaspoon garlic powder	1 teaspoon onion powder
2 tablespoons fresh dill, chopped	2 tablespoons fresh parsley, chopped
Salt and pepper to taste	

Directions:

1. Whirl the Greek yogurt and sour cream in the Cuisinart food processor bowl. 2. Toss in the garlic powder, onion powder, lemon zest, and lemon juice. 3. Blend or process until the mixture reaches a creamy consistency. 4. After adding the parsley and fresh dill, pulse the mixture a few times to combine. 5. Add salt and pepper as desired. 6. After transferring to a serving bowl, allow the flavors to combine by chilling for 30 minutes. 7. Pita chips or fresh veggies are good accompaniments.

CREAMY CORN DIP

Total Time: 15 minutes | Prep Time: 15 minutes

Ingredients:

1 can (15 oz) corn, drained	1 cup cream cheese, softened
1/2 cup sour cream	1 cup shredded cheddar cheese
1/4 cup green onions, chopped	1 tablespoon jalapeño, finely chopped (optional)
Salt and pepper to taste	

Directions:

1. Gather the corn, cream cheese, and sour cream and throw them into the Cuisinart food processor. 2. Blend or process until the mixture reaches a creamy consistency. 3. Consider garnishing with shredded cheddar cheese, green onions, and jalapeño. 4. Pulse till mixed, but with some texture remaining. 5. To taste, season with

salt and pepper. 6. Move to a serving dish and set aside to cool for at least half an hour. 7. Pair with crackers or tortilla chips.

ALMOND COCONUT BALLS

Total Time: 15 minutes | Prep Time: 15 minutes

Ingredients:

1 cup almonds	1 cup shredded coconut (unsweetened)
1/2 cup Medjool dates, pitted	2 tablespoons almond butter
1 teaspoon vanilla extract	A pinch of salt

Directions:

1. Put the almonds in the Cuisinart food processor and pulse until they are finely ground. 2. Toss in the dates, almond butter, salt, vanilla essence, and shredded coconut. 3. The mixture should be processed until it becomes sticky and stays put. 4. Roll the dough into little balls, each about an inch in diameter, using your hands. 5. For added crunch, coat the balls with more shredded coconut. 6. On a tray coated with paper, arrange the balls. 7. Put in the fridge for 30 minutes before you eat it.

ALMOND COCONUT BLISS BARS

Total Time: 25 minutes | Prep Time: 25 minutes

Ingredients:

1 cup almonds	1 cup shredded coconut (unsweetened)
1/2 cup Medjool dates, pitted	1/4 cup maple syrup
1 teaspoon vanilla extract	A pinch of salt

Directions:

1. Almonds and shredded coconut should be mixed together in the food processor that is produced by Cuisinart until the mixture is completely ground. 2. Dates, maple syrup, vanilla essence, and salt should be added to the mixture.

Continue processing until a gooey mixture is formed. 3. Using parchment paper, line a baking dish that is 8 inches by 8 inches. 4. You should press the mixture into the bottom of the dish evenly. 5. For the best results, refrigerate for at least one hour. 6. After it has hardened, cut it into bars. 7. Ensure that the container is sealed and place it in the refrigerator.

DATE ALMOND BARS

Total Time: 20 minutes | Prep Time: 20 minutes

Ingredients:

1 cup Medjool dates, pitted	1 cup almonds
1/2 cup oats	1/4 cup almond butter
1 teaspoon cinnamon	A pinch of salt

Directions:

1. Create a mixture of dates, almonds, and oats by combining them in the Cuisinart food processor to a finely chopped consistency process. 2. The almond butter, cinnamon, and salt should be added, and then the mixture should be processed until it is thoroughly blended. 3. Using parchment paper, line a baking dish that is 8 inches by 8 inches. 4. You should press the mixture into the bottom of the dish evenly. 5. For the best results, refrigerate for at least one hour. 6. After it has become solid, cut it into bars. 7. Place it in an airtight container and keep it at room temperature.

TOMATO BASIL BRUSCHETTA

Total Time: 15 minutes | Prep Time: 15 minutes

Ingredients:

4 ripe tomatoes, chopped	1/4 cup fresh basil leaves
2 cloves garlic, minced	2 tablespoons balsamic vinegar
2 tablespoons olive oil	Salt and pepper to taste

Sliced baguette for serving

Directions:

1. To make the salsa, put the chopped tomatoes, basil leaves, and garlic that have been minced in the Cuisinart food processor. 2. A few pulses will chop the ingredients, but you should still be able to see some texture. 3. First, add the olive oil and balsamic vinegar, and then pulse the mixture to blend. 4. Taste and season with salt and pepper. 5. Place in a dish suitable for serving, and then allow it to sit for ten minutes so that the flavors may combine. 6. Toasted baguette slices should be golden brown in color. 7. On top of the baguette pieces that have been toasted, serve the bruschetta mixture.

TOMATILLO SALSA

Total Time: 15 minutes | Prep Time: 15 minutes

Ingredients:

6-8 tomatillos, husked and rinsed	1 small onion, quartered
1-2 jalapeño peppers, stemmed (remove seeds for less heat)	1 cup fresh cilantro leaves
Juice of 1 lime	Salt to taste

Directions:

1. Please place the tomatillos, onion, and jalapeño peppers into the food processor that is manufactured by Cuisinart. 2. Pulse until extremely finely minced. 3. Add cilantro, lime juice, and salt to the existing mixture. 4. Re-pulse the ingredients until they are thoroughly blended but still have some chunks. 5. Test the seasoning, then make any required adjustments. 6. Place the salsa in a bowl and let it sit for ten minutes so that the flavors continue to combine. 7. You may utilize this as a topping for tacos or serve it with tortilla chips.

PUMPKIN SPICE HUMMUS

Total Time: 10 minutes | Prep Time: 10 minutes

Ingredients:

1 can (15 oz) chickpeas	1 cup canned pumpkin puree
2 tablespoons tahini	2 tablespoons maple syrup
1 teaspoon pumpkin pie spice	1-2 tablespoons lemon juice
Salt to taste	

Directions:

1. The chickpeas, pumpkin puree, tahini, and maple syrup should be mixed together in the food processor that is designed by Cuisinart. 2. Spices of pumpkin pie and lemon juice should be added. 3. The mixture should be processed until it is smooth, with the sides being scraped down as necessary. 4. In order to get the appropriate consistency, add water one tablespoon at a time until the hummus reaches the desired level of thickness. 5. To modify the flavor, taste it and add additional salt and spices if necessary. 6. After transferring to a serving bowl, place in the refrigerator for half an hour. 7. To accompany, pita chips or fresh veggies can be served.

PEANUT BUTTER COOKIE BALLS

Total Time: 15 minutes | Prep Time: 15 minutes

Ingredients:

1 cup natural peanut butter	1 cup rolled oats
1/3 cup honey or maple syrup	1/2 cup chocolate chips
1 teaspoon vanilla extract	Pinch of salt

Directions:

1. Put the peanut butter, oats, honey, vanilla extract, and salt into the Cuisinart food processor and mix them together. 2. The mixture should be processed until it is completely mixed and sticky. 3. Add chocolate chips, then pulse for a few

seconds to combine. 4. When you have a tiny bit of the mixture, scoop it out and roll it into shapes. 5. Group the balls and arrange them on a parchment paper-lined baking sheet. 6. Allow it to chill in the refrigerator for at least half an hour to set. 7. Put it in the refrigerator in a container that can seal out air.

CHOCOLATE ORANGE BALLS

Total Time: 20 minutes | Prep Time: 20 minutes

Ingredients:

1 cup dates, pitted	1 cup almonds (or other nuts)
1/4 cup cocoa powder	Zest of 1 orange
Juice of 1 orange	1/4 teaspoon salt
1/4 cup shredded coconut (optional)	

Directions:

1. It is recommended that the almonds be processed in the Cuisinart food processor until they are finely chopped. 2. Dates, cocoa powder, orange zest, orange juice, and salt should be added to the mixture. 3. The ingredients should be processed until it forms a sticky dough. 4. Form the mixture into balls by scooping out tiny quantities. 5. In order to coat the balls, you might choose to roll them in shredded coconut. 6. After placing the balls on a tray, place them in the refrigerator for at least half an hour. 7. It can be served either cold or at room temperature.

CHOCOLATE PEANUT BITES

Total Time: 25 minutes | Prep Time: 15 minutes

Ingredients:

1 cup roasted peanuts	1/2 cup dark chocolate chips
1 tablespoon coconut oil	1/2 teaspoon vanilla extract
Pinch of sea salt	

Directions:

1. It is necessary to pulse the peanuts in the Cuisinart food processor until they have the consistency of a coarse meal. 2. Coconut oil and chocolate chips can be melted in a double boiler or in a microwave. The peanuts should be added to the food processor along with the chocolate mixture that has been melted. 3. Blend the ingredients until they are thoroughly blended, then add a bit of salt and vanilla essence. 4. Form the mixture into bite-sized balls or bite-sized nibbles using a scoop. 5. Transfer to a parchment paper-lined dish and refrigerate until the cake solidifies. 6. Appreciate either at room temperature or cold.

MOCHA DATE BARS

Total Time: 30 minutes | Prep Time: 15 minutes

Ingredients:

1 cup pitted dates	1 cup rolled oats
1/2 cup nuts (walnuts or almonds)	1 tablespoon instant coffee granules
1/4 cup cocoa powder	Pinch of salt
1 teaspoon vanilla extract	

Directions:

1. To get a finely chopped texture, the nuts should be processed in the Cuisinart food processor. 2. Oats, dates, instant coffee, chocolate powder, salt, and vanilla extract should be added to the mixture. 3. Proceed with the processing until the mixture begins to bind together. 4. Using parchment paper, line a baking dish that is 8 inches by 8 inches. 5. Applying pressure with your hands or a spatula, press the mixture into the dish in an equal manner. 6. Place in the refrigerator for at least fifteen to twenty minutes or until the mixture becomes solid. 7. Cut into bars and serve at room temperature.

CARROT GINGER SOUP

Total Time: 30 minutes | Prep Time: 10 minutes

Ingredients:

1 tablespoon olive oil	1 onion, chopped
2 cloves garlic, minced	1 tablespoon fresh ginger, grated
4 cups carrots, peeled and chopped	4 cups vegetable broth
Salt and pepper to taste	1/2 cup coconut milk (optional)

Directions:

1. With the chopping blade of the Cuisinart Food Processor, cut the onion and garlic until they are perfectly chopped. 2. Sauté onion, garlic, and ginger in olive oil in a large saucepan over medium heat for three minutes to unleash their scent. 3. Mix in the diced carrots and the broth made from vegetables. 4. When carrots are tender, boil, then simmer for 20 minutes. 5. Take the pan from the heat and allow it to cool gently. After adding the soup to the food processor in stages, blend until smooth. 6. The soup should be returned to the stove, seasoned with salt and pepper, and, if preferred, coconut milk could be stirred in. Please bring to a boil before serving.

TOMATO FETA DIP

Total Time: 15 minutes | Prep Time: 5 minutes

Ingredients:

1 can (14 oz) diced tomatoes, drained	1 cup crumbled feta cheese
1/4 cup olive oil	1 tablespoon fresh basil, chopped
Salt and pepper to taste	

Directions:

1. You should put the chopped tomatoes that have been drained, the feta cheese, the olive oil, and the basil in the Cuisinart Food Processor. 2. Process the mixture further until it is well combined and absolutely smooth. 3. Depending on your preference, season with pepper and salt in addition to salt. 4. After placing the dip in a dish for serving, place it in the refrigerator for ten minutes to let the flavors combine. 5. To accompany, pita chips or fresh veggies can be served.

PINEAPPLE COCONUT BITES

Total Time: 20 minutes | Prep Time: 10 minutes

Ingredients:

1 cup dried pineapple, chopped	1 cup shredded coconut
1 cup almonds	1 tablespoon honey (or maple syrup)
1/4 teaspoon salt	

Directions:

1. All of the following ingredients should be combined in the Cuisinart Food Processor: dried pineapple, shredded coconut, almonds, honey, and salt. 2. Process the mixture until it reaches a consistency that is cohesive but still has some texture. 3. Assemble the ingredients into little balls with a diameter of approximately one inch. 4. Place balls on a parchment-lined baking sheet. 5. Put the dish in the refrigerator for ten minutes so that it may be set.

PUMPKIN SPICE BALLS

Total Time: 25 minutes | Prep Time: 15 minutes

Ingredients:

1 cup oats	1/2 cup pumpkin puree
1/2 cup almond butter	1/4 cup honey
1 teaspoon pumpkin pie spice	1/4 cup chocolate chips (optional)

Directions:

1. Oats, pumpkin puree, almond butter, honey, and pumpkin pie spice should be mixed together in the Cuisinart Food Processor. 2. The mixture should be well-mixed and smooth. 3. Use a

spatula to incorporate chocolate chips if you are using them. 4. Assemble the ingredients into little balls with a diameter of approximately one inch. 5. Before serving, place the balls on a dish and place them in the refrigerator for at least ten minutes so that they may get more firm.

GARLIC LEMON HUMMUS

Total Time: 10 minutes | Prep Time: 5 minutes

Ingredients:

1 can (15 oz) chickpeas	1/4 cup tahini
2 tablespoons olive oil	2 cloves garlic, minced
Juice of 1 lemon	Salt to taste
Water as needed for consistency	

Directions:

1. Add chickpeas, tahini, olive oil, garlic, lemon juice, and salt to the Cuisinart Food Processor and process until everything is combined. 2. To get the desired consistency, add water as needed until the mixture is entirely smooth. Test the seasoning, then make any required adjustments. 3. Olive oil should be drizzled over the hummus after it has been transferred to a serving bowl. 4. You may use it as a spread, but you can also serve it with pita.

SMOKY BBQ SAUCE

Total Time: 30 minutes | Prep Time: 10 minutes

Ingredients:

1 cup ketchup	1/4 cup apple cider vinegar
1/4 cup brown sugar	2 tablespoons Worcestershire sauce
2 tablespoons smoked paprika	1 teaspoon garlic powder
1 teaspoon onion powder	1/2 teaspoon cayenne pepper

Salt and pepper to taste

Directions:

1. To make the sauce, throw in some brown sugar, smoked paprika, Worcestershire sauce, ketchup, onion powder, garlic powder, and cayenne pepper in a Cuisinart food processor. 2. Combine all ingredients and process until smooth. 3. Before adding salt and pepper, taste to taste. 4. The sauce should be heated for approximately 10 minutes over medium heat after transferring it to a saucepan. 5. Before using or keeping in the fridge, allow the sauce to cool. 6. Season your preferred grilled meats with this marinade or use it as a dipping sauce.

ALMOND CACAO BALLS

Total Time: 15 minutes | Prep Time: 15 minutes

Ingredients:

1 cup raw almonds	1/2 cup Medjool dates, pitted
1/4 cup unsweetened cocoa powder	1 tablespoon almond butter
1 teaspoon vanilla extract	Pinch of sea salt
Shredded coconut (optional for coating)	

Directions:

1. Toss the almonds into the Cuisinart Food Processor and process until they are finely ground. 2. Almond butter, sea salt, Medjool dates, cocoa powder, and vanilla extract should be mixed together in a food processor after being combined. 3. Mix everything until a sticky dough forms. 4. Form little amounts into balls by scooping them out. 5. Coat the balls with crushed coconut if you want. 6. On a baking sheet lined with paper, set the almond cacao balls. 7. Put in the fridge for 30 minutes before you eat it.

HERB AND LEMON BUTTER

Total Time: 10 minutes | Prep Time: 10 minutes

1 cup unsalted butter, softened	2 tablespoons fresh parsley, chopped
2 tablespoons fresh chives, chopped	1 tablespoon fresh lemon juice
1 teaspoon lemon zest	Salt and pepper to taste

Directions:

1. Prepare the mixture by combining the butter that has been softened, parsley, chives, lemon juice, and lemon zest in the Cuisinart Food Processor. 2. The mixture should be well-mixed and smooth. 3. Before seasoning with salt, add pepper and salt to taste. 4. If necessary, scrape down the sides of the bowl and continue processing the ingredients. 5. After transferring the herb butter to a piece of parchment paper or plastic wrap, let it aside to cool. 6. Refrigerate until it becomes solid, then roll it into a log. 7. Serve on grilled meats, veggies, or toast after being sliced and served.

BLUE CHEESE DIP

Total Time: 10 minutes | Prep Time: 10 minutes

Ingredients:

1 cup sour cream	1/2 cup mayonnaise
1/2 cup crumbled blue cheese	1 tablespoon lemon juice
1 teaspoon Worcestershire sauce	Salt and pepper to taste

Directions:

1. Pour the sour cream, mayonnaise, blue cheese, lemon juice, and Worcestershire sauce into the Cuisinart Food Processor and mix until everything is combined. 2. Process until completely combined, ensuring that some pieces of blue cheese are retained for texture. 3. Taste and adjust with salt and pepper. 4. Place the dip in a dish that is fit for serving. 5. Before serving, allow the dish to chill in the refrigerator for at least half an hour. 6. This may be used as a dressing for salads, alongside fresh veggies, or with chips.

MOCHA HAZELNUT BARS

Total Time: 30 minutes | Prep Time: 15 minutes

Ingredients:

1 cup hazelnuts, toasted	1 cup pitted Medjool dates
1/2 cup rolled oats	1/4 cup unsweetened cocoa powder
1 tablespoon instant coffee granules	1/4 teaspoon sea salt
1/2 cup dark chocolate chips	

Directions:

1. Prepare the roasted hazelnuts by pulsing them in the Cuisinart Food Processor until they are finely ground. 2. Include the rolled oats, cocoa powder, instant coffee granules, and sea salt in the mixture. Add the Medjool dates. 3. The mixture should be processed until it comes together and sticks together when squeezed. 4. Lay the mixture in an even layer on the bottom of an 8-by-8-inch parchment-lined baking dish. 5. After melting dark chocolate chips in a microwave-safe dish, pour them over the hazelnut foundation. 6. Allow the chocolate to set for at least an hour in the refrigerator after spreading it out evenly. 7. Cut into bars and serve at room temperature.

CHOCOLATE ESPRESSO BARS

Total Time: 1 hour | Prep Time: 15 minutes

Ingredients:

1 cup dates, pitted	1 cup almonds
1 cup walnuts	1/4 cup cocoa powder
2 tbsp espresso powder	1/4 cup maple syrup
1/2 tsp vanilla extract	Pinch of salt

Directions:

1. Combine the almonds and walnuts in the Cuisinart Food Processor and process until smooth. Pulse until extremely finely minced. 2. Put in the dates that have been pitted, the cocoa powder, the espresso powder, the maple syrup, the vanilla essence, and the salt. Proceed with the processing until the mixture is well mixed and adheres to itself. 3. Using parchment paper, line a baking dish that is 8 inches by 8 inches. 4. The mixture should be pressed down into the bottom of the dish that has been prepared. 5. Place in the refrigerator for at least half an hour or until the mixture has solidified. 6. Using the parchment paper, remove the bars from the dish after they have reached the desired consistency. 7. Ensure that the container is sealed and place it in the refrigerator.

NUTTY ENERGY BITES

Total Time: 30 minutes | Prep Time: 10 minutes

Ingredients:

1 cup oats	1/2 cup almond butter
1/4 cup honey or maple syrup	1/2 cup mixed nuts (e.g., almonds, walnuts, cashews)
1/4 cup mini chocolate chips	1/4 cup dried fruit (e.g., cranberries or raisins)
1/2 tsp cinnamon	

Directions:

1. Combine the oats, almond butter, honey, and cinnamon in the Cuisinart Food Processor. Process until just combined. Pulse until everything is well combined. 2. Include the chocolate chips, dried fruit, and mixed nuts in the mixture. To combine, give it a couple of quick pulses. 3. Make little balls with your hands, each measuring approximately one inch in diameter. 4. Put the energy bites on a baking sheet that has been lined with parchment paper. 5. Put the mixture in the refrigerator for twenty minutes to

allow it to harden. 6. You may keep it in the refrigerator for up to a week if you store it in an airtight container. 7. Enjoy it as a quick snack or as a boost of energy when you're on the move!

CASHEW COCONUT BITES

Total Time: 25 minutes | Prep Time: 10 minutes

Ingredients:

1 cup cashews	1 cup unsweetened shredded coconut
1/4 cup maple syrup	1/4 cup almond flour
1/2 tsp vanilla extract	Pinch of salt

Directions:

1. The cashews should be pulsed in the Cuisinart Food Processor until they are as finely minced as possible. 2. The shredded coconut, maple syrup, almond flour, vanilla essence, and salt should be added to the coconut mixture. Mix until everything is incorporated and sticky. 3. Scoop out amounts that are about the size of a tablespoon and shape them into balls. 4. Create a single layer of the balls on a baking sheet that has been coated with a sheet of parchment paper. 5. Chill for fifteen minutes so that it can set. 6. You may serve it right away, or you can set it aside in the refrigerator in an airtight container. 7. Consume as a delicious and nutritious snack!

CHERRY ALMOND BALLS

Total Time: 30 minutes | Prep Time: 10 minutes

Ingredients:

1 cup dried cherries	1 cup almonds
1/4 cup almond butter	1/4 cup honey or maple syrup
1/2 tsp almond extract	1/4 cup unsweetened shredded coconut

Directions:

1. The almonds should be combined in the Cuisinart Food Processor and then pulsed until

they are cut into very small pieces. 2. Honey, almond butter, dried cherries, and almond extract should be added to the mixture. Proceed until the ingredients are thoroughly combined. 3. Scoop out amounts that are about the size of a tablespoon and shape them into balls. 4. Each ball should be coated by rolling it in crushed coconut. 5. Put the dough on a baking sheet coated with paper and roll into balls. 6. Put the mixture in the refrigerator for twenty minutes so that it can solidify. 7. Ensure that the container is sealed and place it in the refrigerator.

VEGAN CASHEW CHEESE

Total Time: 10 hours (includes soaking time) | Prep Time: 10 minutes

Ingredients:

1 cup raw cashews	2 tablespoons nutritional yeast
1 tablespoon lemon juice	1 teaspoon garlic powder
1 teaspoon onion powder	1/2 teaspoon salt
1/4 teaspoon black pepper	1-2 tablespoons water (as needed)

Directions:

1. The cashews that have been soaked should be drained and rinsed before being placed in the Cuisinart Food Processor. 2. Nutritional yeast, lemon juice, garlic powder, onion powder, salt, and black pepper should be added to the mixture. 3. The mixture should be processed until it is creamy and smooth, and the sides should be scraped down as necessary. 4. To get the appropriate consistency, add water to the mixture, one tablespoon at a time, until it reaches the desired level of thickness. 5. Taste the seasoning, then make any required adjustments. 6. Before serving, place the cheese in a container and place it in the refrigerator for at least two hours so that it may become more solid. 7. For a spread, crackers, or veggies, this is a delicious option!

CURRY PASTE

Total Time: 15 minutes | Prep Time: 15 minutes

Ingredients:

1/2 cup chopped onion	4 cloves garlic
1 tablespoon fresh ginger, grated	2-3 green chilies (adjust for heat)
1 tablespoon ground coriander	1 tablespoon ground cumin
1 teaspoon turmeric powder	1 tablespoon lime juice
2 tablespoons vegetable oil	Salt to taste

Directions:

1. Start by adding the green chilies, ginger, garlic, and onion to the Cuisinart food processor. 2. As you go, scrape down the edges of the bowl to get a fine chop. 3. Whisk in the cumin, turmeric, ground coriander, lime juice, and vegetable oil. 4. Mince the garlic and onion until a paste forms. Toss in some salt. 5. Freeze the paste for even longer, or move it to an airtight container and refrigerate it for up to seven days. 6. Serve as a foundation for marinades, soups, or curries. 7. Savor the recipes that showcase bright tastes!

ROASTED GARLIC HUMMUS

Total Time: 30 minutes | Prep Time: 10 minutes

Ingredients:

1 can (15 oz) chickpeas	1 head of roasted garlic (squeeze out cloves)
2 tablespoons tahini	2 tablespoons lemon juice
2 tablespoons olive oil	1/2 teaspoon cumin
Salt to taste	Water (as needed for consistency)

Directions:

1. Put the chickpeas, roasted garlic, tahini, lemon juice, olive oil, cumin, and salt into the Cuisinart Food Processor. 2. Scrape down the edges of the bowl as needed to ensure a smooth processing. 3. You may adjust the hummus's thickness by adding a tablespoon of water at a time if it's too thick. 4. Reevaluate the seasoning according to your taste. 5. Spoon the mixture onto a platter and drizzle olive oil over it. 6. Accompany with pita bread, vegetables, or crackers. 7. Put any remaining food in a sealed container and refrigerate it for at least one more day.

ALMOND FIG BITES

Total Time: 15 minutes | Prep Time: 15 minutes

Ingredients:

1 cup raw almonds	1 cup dried figs, stems removed
1 tablespoon chia seeds (optional)	1/4 teaspoon salt
1 tablespoon maple syrup or honey (optional)	

Directions:

1. Pulse finely chopped raw almonds in a Cuisinart food processor to make them. 2. Season with salt and stir in the dried figs and chia seeds if using. Continue processing until a dough forms. 3. To adjust the consistency, add honey or maple syrup and pulse one more until well blended. 4. Press the mixture onto a prepared baking tray to make bars, or roll it into little balls. 5. To set, chill for half an hour. 6. Refrigerate for a maximum of two weeks if stored in an airtight container. 7. For a fast pick-me-up or snack, try these!

SPICY THAI SAUCE

Total Time: 10 minutes | Prep Time: 10 minutes

Ingredients:

1/4 cup peanut butter	Two tablespoons soy sauce or tamari
1 tablespoon lime juice	One tablespoon of maple syrup or honey
1-2 teaspoons sriracha (adjust for spice level)	1 tablespoon sesame oil
Water (as needed for consistency)	

Directions:

1. Peanut butter, soy sauce, lime juice, maple syrup, sriracha, and sesame oil should all be mixed together in a Cuisinart food processor. 2. Add water as needed to get the desired consistency and process until smooth. 3. Adjust the sweetness or spice level to your liking by tasting. 4. Spoon into a jar and refrigerate for a week or more. 5. Dip veggies in it, toss salads with it or use it as a sauce for noodles. 6. Savor the robust flavors in your food! 7. Feel free to play around with other spices or ingredients to make the sauce your own.

LEMON COCONUT BARS

Total Time: 1 hour | Prep Time: 20 minutes

Ingredients:

1 cup all-purpose flour	½ cup powdered sugar
½ cup unsalted butter, softened	1 cup granulated sugar
3 large eggs	½ cup fresh lemon juice
1 tablespoon lemon zest	1 cup shredded coconut
¼ teaspoon salt	Powdered sugar for dusting (optional)

Directions:

1. Aim for 175°C, or 350°F, in the oven. Coat an 8-by-8-inch baking dish with a thin coating of oil. 2. Fill the Cuisinart food processor with the melted butter, then add the flour and powdered sugar. 3. The mixture should look like coarse crumbs after pulsing. 4. In the bottom of the

baking dish that you have prepared, press the crumb mixture. Cook for 15 minutes or until a slight golden color appears. 5. Eggs, granulated sugar, lemon zest, coconut, and salt should all be blended together in a food processor until completely creamy. 6. After the crust has baked, pour the lemon mixture on top and put it back in the oven. Continue baking for another quarter of an hour. 7. After taking it out of the oven, allow it to cool entirely on the pan. After that, sprinkle with powdered sugar and cut into bars.

HERB-INFUSED OIL

Total Time: 1 hour (plus steeping time) | Prep Time: 10 minutes

Ingredients:

1 cup olive oil	½ cup fresh herbs (basil, rosemary, thyme, or your choice)
2 cloves garlic, crushed (optional)	½ teaspoon red pepper flakes (optional)

Directions:

1. Olive oil, fresh herbs, garlic, and freshly ground red pepper flakes should be mixed together in a small pot. 2. Allow the mixture to be heated over low heat for around twenty minutes, enabling the flavors to combine without allowing it to boil. 3. The oil should be removed from the heat and allowed to cool to room temperature. 4. The sediments should be discarded once the oil has been strained through a fine mesh filter and poured into a clean container. 5. The food may be kept in the refrigerator for up to a month. Before you use it, make sure it has reached room temperature.

COCONUT MINT CHUTNEY

Total Time: 15 minutes | Prep Time: 15 minutes

Ingredients:

1 cup fresh mint leaves	1 cup shredded coconut (fresh or unsweetened)
2 green chilies, chopped	1 tablespoon lemon juice
Salt to taste	

Directions:

1. The Cuisinart Food Processor should be loaded with the following Ingredients: mint leaves, shredded coconut, green chilies, lemon juice, and salt. 2. Pulse them until they are finely minced and well mixed. 3. In order to produce a smooth consistency, you may need to add a small bit of water. 4. You can vary the amount of salt or lemon juice according to your taste. 5. In a serving bowl, transfer the mixture, and serve it either as a condiment or with snacks.

RASPBERRY COCONUT BALLS

Total Time: 30 minutes | Prep Time: 20 minutes

Ingredients:

1 cup almond flour	½ cup shredded coconut
½ cup fresh raspberries (or freeze-dried raspberries)	2 tablespoons maple syrup
1 teaspoon vanilla extract	

Directions:

1. Combine the following ingredients in the Cuisinart Food Processor: almond flour, shredded coconut, raspberries, maple syrup, and vanilla essence. Enjoy! 2. After the mixture has been well mixed and is sticky, pulse it. 3. You can use your hands to shape the mixture into little balls with a diameter of approximately one inch! 4. To chill the balls for at least ten minutes, place them on a tray that has been lined with parchment paper. 5. After chilling, serve or keep in the refrigerator for up to a week in an airtight container.

WALNUT CRANBERRY BALLS

Total Time: 25 minutes | Prep Time: 15 minutes

Ingredients:

1 cup walnuts	½ cup dried cranberries
¼ cup maple syrup	1 teaspoon vanilla extract
Pinch of salt	

Directions:

1. The walnuts should be pulsed in the Cuisinart Food Processor until they are finely ground but not crushed to the point where they resemble flour. 2. When the walnuts have been pulverized, add the dried cranberries, maple syrup, vanilla essence, and salt respectively. 3. The mixture should be well mixed and sticky after being pulsed. 4. With the help of your hands, form the mixture into little balls that are approximately one inch in diameter. 5. To prepare the balls for serving, place them on a platter and place them in the refrigerator for at least ten minutes.

WHITE CHEDDAR DIP

Total Time: 15 minutes | Prep Time: 15 minutes

Ingredients:

1 cup white cheddar cheese, shredded	1 cup cream cheese, softened
1/2 cup sour cream	2 tablespoons mayonnaise
1 tablespoon Worcestershire sauce	1 teaspoon garlic powder
1 teaspoon onion powder	Salt and pepper to taste
Fresh chives for garnish (optional)	

Directions:

1. Mix the white cheddar cheese, cream cheese, sour cream, and mayonnaise together in a food processor made by Cuisinart. 2. Salt and pepper, then add garlic, onion, Worcestershire sauce, and the mixture. 3. While doing so, scrape down the sides of the bowl as necessary. Process until the mixture reaches a velvety consistency. 4. Test the seasoning, then make any required adjustments. 5. The dip should be transferred to a serving bowl, and if desired, fresh chives may be used as a garnish. 6. Put in the fridge until you're ready to eat, or go ahead and pile on the chips, crackers, or fresh vegetables right now. Alternatively, serve immediately.

ALMOND MAYONNAISE

Total Time: 10 minutes | Prep Time: 10 minutes

Ingredients:

1 cup raw almonds, blanched	1 tablespoon lemon juice
1 teaspoon Dijon mustard	1/2 teaspoon salt
1/2 cup water (more as needed)	

Directions:

1. Grind the blanched almonds to a fine powder in a Cuisinart food processor. 2. Combine the salt, Dijon mustard, lemon juice, and lemon zest. 3. Add the water little by little while the machine is running until the mixture is creamy and smooth. 4. To thin down the mayonnaise, add a tablespoon of water at a time until it reaches the consistency you like. 5. See whether the seasoning needs adjusting by tasting. 6. Put the almond mayonnaise in a sealed container and put it in the fridge. 7. Spread or dress as soon as possible; use within a week.

PEANUT BUTTER ENERGY BALLS

Total Time: 15 minutes | Prep Time: 15 minutes

Ingredients:

1 cup rolled oats	1/2 cup natural peanut butter
1/4 cup honey or maple syrup	1/4 cup ground flaxseed

1/2 cup chocolate chips or raisins

1 teaspoon vanilla extract

A pinch of salt

Directions:

1. Put the peanut butter, honey, rolled oats, ground flaxseed, chocolate chips, vanilla extract, and salt into the Cuisinart food processor. 2. To make a sticky dough, pulse the ingredients until they are thoroughly mixed. 3. Just a touch of extra peanut butter or honey, and the combination will be just right. 4. Roll into little balls, each approximately an inch in diameter, using your hands. 5. Spread out the energy balls on a parchment-lined baking sheet. 6. Put in the fridge for 30 minutes to set. 7. Put in a sealed jar and refrigerate for no more than a week.

DIJON MUSTARD VINAIGRETTE

Total Time: 5 minutes | Prep Time: 5 minutes

Ingredients:

1/4 cup Dijon mustard

1/4 cup red wine vinegar

1/2 cup olive oil

1 teaspoon honey (optional)

Salt and pepper to taste

Directions:

1. Dijon mustard and red wine vinegar should be mixed together in the food processor, which is Cuisinart, and then processed. 2. To ensure proper incorporation, add the olive oil slowly and steadily while the machine is operating. 3. In the event that you are using honey, add it to taste and pulse it to blend. 4. Depending on your preference, season with salt and pepper. 5. Make any required adjustments to the sweetness or seasoning based on your taste. 6. It is recommended that the vinaigrette be transferred to a jar and shaken thoroughly before serving. 7. Take care to shake the container before each use and store it in the refrigerator for up to two weeks.

VEGAN MAC AND CHEESE SAUCE

Total Time: 20 minutes | Prep Time: 10 minutes

Ingredients:

1 cup raw cashews

1/4 cup nutritional yeast

1/4 cup water

1 tablespoon lemon juice

1 teaspoon garlic powder

1 teaspoon onion powder

1 teaspoon mustard (Dijon or yellow)

Salt and pepper to taste

Directions:

1. Combine the cashews that have been soaked and then drained, nutritional yeast, water, lemon juice, garlic powder, onion powder, and mustard in your Cuisinart food processor. 2. On high speed, blend until the mixture is completely smooth and creamy, scraping down the edges as necessary. 3. You may adjust the spice as necessary and add salt and pepper to taste. 4. You may adjust the consistency of the sauce by adding additional water, one tablespoon at a time until you reach the appropriate level of thickness. 5. Use it as a dip for veggies or serve it warm over pasta that has already been cooked.

HAZELNUT FUDGE BALLS

Total Time: 30 minutes | Prep Time: 15 minutes

Ingredients:

1 cup raw hazelnuts

1 cup Medjool dates, pitted

1/4 cup cocoa powder

1/2 teaspoon vanilla extract

A pinch of salt

Additional crushed hazelnuts for rolling (optional)

Directions:

1. Use your Cuisinart food processor to pulse the hazelnuts until they are chopped into a finer consistency. 2. The processor should be filled with pitted dates, cocoa powder, vanilla essence, and salt. 3. The mixture should be processed until it is completely mixed and sticky. 4. Scoop out amounts that are about the size of a tablespoon and shape them into balls. 5. For an additional layer of texture, you might choose to roll the balls in crushed hazelnuts. 6. If you want to serve the balls, place them on a platter and put them in the refrigerator for at least fifteen minutes.

CURRY COCONUT DIP

Total Time: 15 minutes | Prep Time: 10 minutes

Ingredients:

1 cup canned coconut milk	2 tablespoons curry powder
1 tablespoon lime juice	1 teaspoon garlic powder
Salt to taste	Fresh cilantro for garnish (optional)

Directions:

1. Add the coconut milk, curry powder, lime juice, garlic powder, and salt to your Cuisinart food processor and pulse until everything is combined. 2. The mixture should be smooth and creamy. 3. Take a taste, and if required, adjust the seasoning. 4. Move the dip to a dish ready for serving. 5. Accompany with pita chips or a side of fresh vegetables; optionally, top with chopped cilantro.

CRANBERRY WALNUT BALLS

Total Time: 25 minutes | Prep Time: 15 minutes

Ingredients:

1 cup walnuts	1 cup dried cranberries
1/2 cup rolled oats	1 tablespoon maple syrup

1 teaspoon vanilla extract	A pinch of salt

Directions:

1. Use your Cuisinart food processor to pulse the walnuts until they are chopped into a finer consistency. 2. Salt, maple syrup, vanilla essence, and dried cranberries should be added to the food processor. Rolling oats should also be included. 3. Incorporate all of the ingredients while retaining some texture by blending them until smooth. 4. Scoop out amounts that are about the size of a tablespoon and shape them into balls. 5. Before serving, remove the balls from the refrigerator and place them on a dish. Allow them to chill for ten minutes.

ALMOND JOY BITES

Total Time: 25 minutes | Prep Time: 15 minutes

Ingredients:

1 cup Medjool dates, pitted	1 cup unsweetened shredded coconut
1/2 cup almond butter	1/4 cup cocoa powder
1/4 cup whole almonds	A pinch of salt

Directions:

1. The dates that have been pitted, the shredded coconut, the almond butter, the cocoa powder, and the salt should be mixed together in your Cuisinart food processor. 2. The mixture should be blended until it is smooth and sticky. 3. Scoop out chunks that are about the size of a tablespoon and flatten them into discs. 4. To make a ball out of the mixture, place a whole almond in the middle of each disc and then wrap the mixture around the almond. 5. Place the bits on a platter, and then place them in the refrigerator for fifteen minutes so that they can set.

APRICOT COCONUT BALLS

Total Time: 20 minutes | Prep Time: 10 minutes

Ingredients:

1 cup dried apricots	1 cup unsweetened shredded coconut
1/2 cup almonds (or any nut of your choice)	1 tablespoon maple syrup
A pinch of salt	

Directions:

1. After combining the dried apricots, shredded coconut, almonds, maple syrup, and salt in your Cuisinart food processor, proceed to process the mixture. 2. When everything is combined and sticky, stop blending. 3. Scoop out amounts that are about the size of a tablespoon and shape them into balls. 4. Should you so wish, you may cover the balls with extra shredded coconut by rolling them in it. 5. The dish should be placed on a platter and then chilled for ten minutes before being served.

CHEESY GARLIC SPREAD

Total Time: 10 minutes | Prep Time: 10 minutes

Ingredients:

8 oz cream cheese, softened	1 cup shredded cheddar cheese
2 cloves garlic, minced	1 tablespoon fresh chives, chopped
1 tablespoon fresh parsley, chopped	Salt and pepper to taste

Directions:

1. The cream cheese that has been softened and the shredded cheddar cheese should be mixed together in your Cuisinart home food processor bowl. 2. Please add the chopped parsley, chopped chives, and minced garlic to the mixture. 3. Before seasoning with salt, add pepper and salt to taste. 4. Keep doing this until the ingredients are completely combined and creamy. 5. Test the seasoning, then make any required adjustments. 6. Transfer to a bowl designed for serving, and place in the refrigerator for at least half an hour before serving. 7. To accompany, crackers, bread, or fresh veggies can be served.

MINTED YOGURT SAUCE

Total Time: 10 minutes | Prep Time: 10 minutes

Ingredients:

1 cup plain yogurt (Greek or regular)	1/4 cup fresh mint leaves
1 clove garlic, minced	1 tablespoon lemon juice
Salt to taste	

Directions:

1. Mix the plain yogurt, fresh mint leaves, and minced garlic in your Cuisinart food processor until everything is combined. 2. It would be good to add a pinch of salt and a squeeze of lemon. 3. Pulse it to ensure that the mixture is completely smooth and the mint is finely chopped. 4. Taste, then make any necessary adjustments to the salt. 5. Move the mixture to a dish for serving. 6. Refrigerate the mixture for at least half an hour with the lid on to enable the flavors to combine. 7. Use this condiment as a dipping sauce for veggies or a sauce for grilled meats.

SALSA VERDE

Total Time: 15 minutes | Prep Time: 10 minutes

Ingredients:

1 cup fresh cilantro leaves	1/2 cup fresh parsley leaves
1/4 cup lime juice	1 jalapeño, seeds removed (optional)
2 cloves garlic	Salt to taste
Olive oil (optional for thinning)	

Directions:

1. Take the cilantro leaves, parsley leaves, lime juice, jalapeño, and garlic and place them in the bowl of your Cuisinart food processor. 2. Pulse

them to ensure that the herbs are finely minced. 3. Re-pulse the ingredients to blend them, then add salt to taste. 4. During the time that the food processor is operating, sprinkle in olive oil if you would like the consistency to be thinner. 5. Taste the seasoning, then make any required adjustments. 6. Move the mixture to a dish for serving. 7. Serve alongside tacos, tortilla chips, or meats that have been grilled.

CHOCOLATE PISTACHIO BALLS

Total Time: 20 minutes | Prep Time: 15 minutes

Ingredients:

1 cup pitted dates	1 cup roasted pistachios
1/4 cup unsweetened cocoa powder	1 teaspoon vanilla extract
A pinch of salt	Additional chopped pistachios for coating

Directions:

1. Put the dates that have been pitted, the pistachios that have been roasted, the cocoa powder, the vanilla essence, and the salt into your Cuisinart food processor. 2. The ingredients should be pulsed until thoroughly blended, and a sticky dough should be produced. 3. Form the mixture into balls by scooping out sections of it that are about the size of a tablespoon. 4. Pistachios that have been chopped should be used to coat each ball before rolling it. 5. Put the chocolate pistachio balls on a tray that has been lined with parchment paper. 6. Put in the refrigerator for at least one hour to thicken. 7. Serve chilled as a sweet snack or dessert; serve chilled.

FRESH TOMATO MARINARA

Total Time: 30 minutes | Prep Time: 10 minutes

Ingredients:

4 cups ripe tomatoes, chopped	1/4 cup olive oil
4 cloves garlic, minced	1 teaspoon dried oregano
1 teaspoon salt	Fresh basil leaves for garnish

Directions:

1. The chopped tomatoes should be pulsed in your Cuisinart food processor until they are roughly mixed (the consistency may be adjusted to achieve the desired consistency). 2. The olive oil will work best if heated in a large skillet over medium heat. 3. Sauté the minced garlic for a minute or two after adding it to the pan. 4. Put the tomatoes that have been pureed into the skillet, then add the oregano and salt and whisk everything together. 5. For fifteen to twenty minutes, allow the sauce to boil while stirring it occasionally. 6. Test the seasoning, then make any required adjustments. 7. Before serving as a dipping sauce or as a topping for pasta, garnish with fresh basil leaves.

CARAMELIZED ONION DIP

Total Time: 45 minutes | Prep Time: 10 minutes

Ingredients:

2 large onions, thinly sliced	2 tablespoons olive oil
1 teaspoon salt	1 cup sour cream
1 cup cream cheese, softened	1 teaspoon garlic powder
1 teaspoon Worcestershire sauce	Fresh chives, for garnish

Directions:

1. Before using a Cuisinart food processor, bring the olive oil to a simmer in a pan located over medium heat. The sliced onions and salt should be added. 2. It should take around half an hour for the onions to get caramelized and golden brown, during which time they should be stirred constantly. Take the pan off the heat and let it cool. 3. The caramelized onions should be combined with sour cream, cream cheese, garlic powder, and Worcestershire sauce in the food

processor. The onions should be allowed to cool. 4. Check the seasoning with a taste before continuing to process until the mixture reaches a velvety smoothness. 5. Transfer the dip to a dish that is suitable for serving, and then top it with chopped chives. 6. You may serve this dish with chips, crackers, or veggie sticks.

FRESH HERB TARTAR SAUCE

Total Time: 15 minutes | Prep Time: 15 minutes

Ingredients:

1 cup mayonnaise	1 tablespoon Dijon mustard
2 tablespoons lemon juice	1 tablespoon capers, rinsed and chopped
1 tablespoon fresh parsley, chopped	1 tablespoon fresh dill, chopped
Salt and pepper to taste	

Directions:

1. Mayonnaise, Dijon mustard, lemon juice, and minced capers should be mixed together in the food processor that is available from Cuisinart. 2. Additionally, season the dish with salt and pepper, and then add the chopped parsley and dill. 3. Pulse the ingredients until the herbs are chopped very small, and the mixture is thoroughly blended. 4. Taste the seasoning, then make any required adjustments. 5. Once the tartar sauce has been transferred to a bowl, it should be chilled for at least half an hour before being served. 6. Serve as a dip for vegetables, fish, or shellfish or as a condiment for fish.

MOCHA MINT BITES

Total Time: 30 minutes | Prep Time: 15 minutes

Ingredients:

1 cup dates, pitted	1 cup walnuts
1/4 cup cocoa powder	1 tablespoon espresso powder
1/4 teaspoon peppermint extract	1/4 cup unsweetened shredded coconut (optional)

Directions:

1. Both the dates and the walnuts should be mixed together in the Cuisinart food processor. To make coarse crumbs, pulse all of the ingredients together. 2. Cocoa powder, espresso powder, and peppermint essence should be added to the mixture. The mixture should be processed until it is completely mixed and sticky. 3. Make bite-sized balls out of the mixture by scooping out tiny parts of it and rolling them into balls. 4. In order to coat the balls, you might choose to roll them in shredded coconut. 5. To allow the bites to set, place them on a tray that has been lined with parchment paper and place it in the refrigerator for at least fifteen minutes. 6. Serve cold, and have pleasure in it!

GINGER MISO DRESSING

Total Time: 10 minutes | Prep Time: 10 minutes

Ingredients:

1/4 cup white miso paste	2 tablespoons rice vinegar
2 tablespoons sesame oil	1 tablespoon fresh ginger, grated
1 tablespoon honey or maple syrup	1-2 tablespoons water (to thin, if necessary)

Directions:

1. Miso paste, rice vinegar, sesame oil, grated ginger, and honey should be mixed together in the food processor that is manufactured by Cuisinart. 2. Keep going until everything is well combined and blended. 3. In order to get the appropriate consistency, add water one tablespoon at a time until the dressing reaches the desired level of thickness. 4. The seasoning should be tasted and adjusted as necessary, with additional honey being added for sweetness if required. 5. Put the dressing in a jar or other container, and store it in the refrigerator until

you are ready to use it. 6. Serve as a dip, on top of salads, or on veggies that have been grilled.

CASHEW CHEESE SPREAD

Total Time: 15 minutes | Prep Time: 15 minutes

Ingredients:

1 cup raw cashews	2 tablespoons nutritional yeast
2 tablespoons lemon juice	1 clove garlic
1 teaspoon onion powder	1/2 teaspoon salt
Water (as needed for consistency)	

Directions:

1. Cashews that have been soaked, nutritional yeast, lemon juice, garlic, onion powder, and salt should be mixed together together in the Cuisinart Food Processor. 2. The mixture should be processed until it is smooth, with the sides being scraped down as necessary. 3. When you achieve the correct consistency, add water one tablespoon at a time until you have attained it. 4. Test the seasoning, then make any required adjustments. 5. Put the mixture into a dish designed for serving, and then refrigerate it for at least half an hour before serving. 6. Spread it on sandwiches, serve it with crackers, or serve it with vegetables.

ROASTED PINEAPPLE SALSA

Total Time: 30 minutes | Prep Time: 10 minutes

Ingredients:

1 medium ripe pineapple, peeled	1/2 red onion, diced
1 red bell pepper, diced	1 jalapeño, seeds removed and minced
2 tablespoons fresh cilantro, chopped	Juice of 1 lime
Salt to taste	

Directions:

1. Roast the vegetables until they are soft, about 20 minutes before serving. 2. Put the pineapple pieces on a baking sheet and roast them for fifteen to twenty minutes or until they have a caramelized appearance. 3. Put the roasted pineapple, red onion, red bell pepper, jalapeño, cilantro, lime juice, and salt into the Cuisinart Food Processor. Mix all of these ingredients together. 4. It should be merged, but it should still be chunky. 5. Test the seasoning, then make any required adjustments. 6. Either serve it warm or cold with tortilla chips or use it as a topping for meats that have been grilled.

COCONUT FIG BARS

Total Time: 45 minutes | Prep Time: 15 minutes

Ingredients:

1 cup dried figs, stems removed	1 cup rolled oats
1 cup shredded coconut	1/2 cup almond butter
1/4 cup honey or maple syrup	1 teaspoon vanilla extract
Pinch of salt	

Directions:

1. Butter and flour a baking dish that is 8 by 8 inches and set the oven temperature to 350 degrees Fahrenheit. 2. Put the figs, oats, coconut, almond butter, honey, vanilla, and salt into the Cuisinart Food Processor and mix till everything is combined. 3. The ingredients should be processed until they are thoroughly incorporated and form a sticky dough. 4. In the baking dish that has been prepared, press the mixture down firmly. 5. To get a golden brown color, bake for 25 to 30 minutes. 6. Before cutting into bars, wait until the bar has totally cooled down. 7. Ensure that the container is sealed and place it in the refrigerator.

GINGER SPICE BARS

Total Time: 50 minutes | Prep Time: 15 minutes

Ingredients:

1 cup all-purpose flour	1 teaspoon baking powder
1 teaspoon ground ginger	1/2 teaspoon cinnamon
1/4 teaspoon nutmeg	1/4 teaspoon salt
1/2 cup unsalted butter, softened	1 cup brown sugar
1 egg	1 tablespoon fresh ginger, grated

Directions:

1. Grease an 8-by-8-inch baking pan and set the oven temperature to 350°F (175°C). 2. Grinding ginger, cinnamon, nutmeg, baking powder, salt, and flour should all be pulsed together in a Cuisinart food processor. 3. Beat the brown sugar and butter until they are light and frothy in another bowl. 4. After you've mixed in the egg, add the grated fresh ginger. 5. Combine the dry components with the wet ones in a slow, steady stream. 6. Use the prepared baking sheet to pour the ingredients. 30–35 minutes in the oven should be enough time for a toothpick to emerge clean when put in the center. After cooling, cut into squares.

MAPLE WALNUT BARS

Total Time: 45 minutes | Prep Time: 15 minutes

Ingredients:

1 cup walnuts, chopped	1 cup rolled oats
1/2 cup almond flour	1/2 cup maple syrup
1/4 cup coconut oil, melted	1 teaspoon vanilla extract
Pinch of salt	

Directions:

1. Arrange parchment paper in an 8x8-inch baking dish and preheat the oven to 350°F, which is 175°C. 2. Almond flour, walnuts, maple syrup, melted coconut oil, salt, and vanilla should all be mixed together in the Cuisinart food processor. 3. Mix until mixed, but with some visible chunks. 4. After filling the baking dish, push down firmly to compact the mixture. 5. To get golden brown edges, bake for 25 to 30 minutes. 6. Let it cool entirely before cutting it into bars. 7. Keep at room temperature in a sealed container.

APRICOT ALMOND BITES

Total Time: 15 minutes | Prep Time: 15 minutes

Ingredients:

1 cup dried apricots	1 cup almonds
1/2 cup shredded coconut (unsweetened)	1 tablespoon honey or maple syrup
1 teaspoon vanilla extract	A pinch of salt

Directions:

1. Paste the almonds and dried apricots into the Cuisinart food processor. Chop them finely by pulsing. 2. Toss in the salt, honey (or maple syrup), shredded coconut, and vanilla essence. The mixture will begin to clump together after processing. 3. Divide the mixture into tablespoon-sized parts and shape them into balls. 4. Divide the mixture into balls and place them on a baking sheet coated with paper. 5. Before serving, let it firm up in the fridge for at least half an hour. 6. Put any remaining food in a sealed container and refrigerate it for at least one more day.

GARLIC PARMESAN PESTO

Total Time: 10 minutes | Prep Time: 10 minutes

Ingredients:

2 cups fresh basil leaves	1/4 cup pine nuts
2 cloves garlic	1/2 cup grated Parmesan cheese

1/2 cup olive oil   Salt and pepper to taste

Directions:

1. Put the garlic, pine nuts, and basil leaves in a food processor. Chop into tiny pieces by pulsing. 2. After you scrape the bowl's sides, add the shredded Parmesan cheese. 3. Add the olive oil little by little while the processor is running to get a creamy pesto. 4. To taste, season with salt and pepper. Put the pesto in a jar and keep it in the fridge for a week. 5. Spread it on, dip it, or stir it into your spaghetti.

BLUEBERRY BLISS BARS

Total Time: 30 minutes | Prep Time: 15 minutes

Ingredients:

1 cup rolled oats	1/2 cup almond flour
1/4 cup honey or maple syrup	1/4 cup almond butter
1 cup fresh or frozen blueberries	1/2 teaspoon cinnamon
A pinch of salt	

Directions:

1. Prepare a baking pan measuring 8 inches by 8 inches with parchment paper and pre-heat the oven to 350°F. 2. Melt the almond butter, cinnamon, salt, honey (or maple syrup), rolled oats, and almond flour in a food processor. Blend everything together until smooth. 3. Using a spatula, gently incorporate the blueberries. 4. Once the baking pan is ready, press the mixture evenly into it. 5. To get golden brown edges, bake for around fifteen to twenty minutes. 6. After baking, allow it to cool completely in the pan before slicing. 7. Keep for up to a week in a sealed jar at room temperature.

VANILLA DATE BALLS

Total Time: 10 minutes | Prep Time: 10 minutes

Ingredients:

1 cup pitted Medjool dates	1 cup walnuts or almonds
1/4 cup shredded coconut (unsweetened)	1 teaspoon vanilla extract
A pinch of salt	

Directions:

1. Pitted dates and nuts should be combined in a food processor. Mix until the mixture is sticky and coarsely chopped. 2. Combine the salt, vanilla essence, and shredded coconut. Blend the ingredients together by pulsing the mixture. 3. Form the mixture into balls using spoonfuls. 4. If you want to add some flair, roll the balls in some more shredded coconut. 5. To make them firmer, put the date balls on a dish and put them in the fridge for half an hour. 6. Refrigerate for a maximum of two weeks if stored in an airtight container.

CHAI SPICE BARS

Total Time: 45 minutes | Prep Time: 15 minutes

Ingredients:

1 ½ cups almond flour	1 cup rolled oats
½ cup maple syrup	½ cup coconut oil, melted
1 teaspoon vanilla extract	1 teaspoon ground cinnamon
½ teaspoon ground ginger	¼ teaspoon ground cardamom
¼ teaspoon ground cloves	¼ teaspoon salt

Directions:

1. Start the oven higher to warm to 350°F (175°C). 2. Use parchment paper to line an 8-by-8-inch baking dish. 3. Add the almond flour, rolled oats, salt, cinnamon, ginger, cardamom, and cloves to the Cuisinart Food Processor. Mix by pulsing. 4. Combine the maple syrup, vanilla

essence, and melted coconut oil. Mix until a dough that sticks together develops. 5. Make sure that the mixture is evenly distributed across the baking dish that has been prepared. Use a spatula to even out the surface. 6. To get a golden brown color, bake for 25 to 30 minutes. After it has cooled, cut it into bars.

PEANUT BUTTER BROWNIE BALLS

Total Time: 20 minutes | Prep Time: 10 minutes

Ingredients:

1 cup pitted dates	½ cup peanut butter
½ cup cocoa powder	1 teaspoon vanilla extract
½ cup rolled oats	Pinch of salt
Optional: chopped nuts or coconut for rolling	

Directions:

1. Blend the dates in the Cuisinart Food Processor until they come together to make a sticky paste. 2. Rolling oats, peanut butter, cocoa powder, vanilla essence, and salt should be added to the mixture. Pulse until everything is well blended. 3. Assemble the ingredients into little balls with a diameter of approximately one inch. 4. Should you so wish, you may coat the balls by rolling them in chopped nuts or coconut. 5. Before serving, place the mixture in the refrigerator for half an hour to allow it to become more solid.

COCONUT ALMOND JOY BARS

Total Time: 30 minutes | Prep Time: 15 minutes

Ingredients:

1 cup almond flour	1 cup shredded unsweetened coconut
½ cup almond butter	¼ cup maple syrup
1 teaspoon vanilla extract	½ cup dark chocolate chips

Directions:

1. Put the shredded coconut and almond flour into the Cuisinart Food Processor and mix them together. Mix thoroughly by pulsing. 2. Include vanilla essence, maple syrup, and almond butter in the mixture. Keep processing until a dough is formed. 3. Prepare an 8x8-inch baking dish lined with parchment paper and press the ingredients onto it evenly. 4. Combine the water and dark chocolate chips in a microwave-safe bowl or over a double boiler. Over the bars, drizzle or distribute the mixture. 5. Place in the refrigerator for fifteen minutes or until the chocolate has hardened. Once you are ready to serve, cut into squares.

CHARRED TOMATO SALSA

Total Time: 20 minutes | Prep Time: 10 minutes

Ingredients:

4 medium tomatoes, halved	1 jalapeño, halved (seeds removed for less heat)
1 small onion, quartered	2 cloves garlic, unpeeled
1 tablespoon olive oil	¼ cup fresh cilantro
Juice of 1 lime	Salt to taste

Directions:

1. Set a grill or a skillet over medium-high heat and get it ready to use. Olive oil should be used to toss the tomatoes, jalapeño, onion, and garlic together. 2. The veggies should be grilled or charred for around eight to ten minutes, turning them regularly until they have been scorched and softened. 3. Take the veggies that have been charred off the flame and let them cool down a little bit. 4. Add charred veggies, cilantro, lime juice, and salt to the Cuisinart Food Processor and process until everything is combined. Pulse the ingredients until they achieve the ideal consistency. 5. Serve immediately with tortilla

chips, or keep in the refrigerator for up to a week. Serve immediately.

COCONUT PISTACHIO FUDGE BARS

Total Time: 30 minutes | Prep Time: 15 minutes

Ingredients:

2 cups shredded unsweetened coconut	1 cup pistachios, shelled
½ cup maple syrup	½ cup coconut oil, melted
1 teaspoon vanilla extract	

Directions:

1. Prepare the pistachios by blending them in the Cuisinart Food Processor until they are finely pulverized but not paste-like. 2. The ingredients that should be included are shredded coconut, maple syrup, melted coconut oil, and vanilla essence. Mix well by pulsing the ingredients. 3. After pressing the mixture into an 8-by-8-inch parchment-lined baking dish, level it with a spatula. 4. 15 minutes in the refrigerator until the mixture has set. Once the substance has settled, cut it into bars. 5. When stored in a container that is airtight, it may be kept in the refrigerator for up to a week.

CASHEW ALFREDO SAUCE

Total Time: 10 minutes | Prep Time: 5 minutes

Ingredients:

1 cup raw cashews	1 cup almond milk
2 tablespoons nutritional yeast	1 tablespoon lemon juice
1 teaspoon garlic powder	½ teaspoon salt
Black pepper to taste	

Directions:

1. Drain and rinse the cashews after they have been soaked. For best results, process them in a Cuisinart food processor. 2. The following items should be mixed: nutritional yeast, almond milk, salt, black pepper, lemon juice, and garlic powder. 3. To get a creamy, smooth consistency, blend the ingredients until the bowl is clean, stopping to scrape down the sides as needed. 4. Simply add more almond milk if you like a thinner sauce. Keep repeating this until the sauce gets to the consistency you want it to. 5. The sauce may be served immediately over pasta or veggies, or it can be kept in the fridge for up to nine days.

VANILLA NUT BITES

Total Time: 30 minutes | Prep Time: 10 minutes

Ingredients:

1 cup raw almonds	1 cup pitted Medjool dates
1 teaspoon vanilla extract	1/4 teaspoon sea salt
1/2 cup shredded unsweetened coconut (optional)	

Directions:

1. Make careful to pulse the almonds until they are finely chopped after adding them to the Cuisinart food processor. 2. Combine the chopped almonds with the dates, vanilla essence, and sea salt. Once the ingredients are combined and sticky, process the mixture. 3. If using shredded coconut, stir it into the mixture with a spatula. 4. Line a baking dish with parchment paper. For the mixture to settle into the dish's base, push down firmly. 5. After about twenty minutes in the fridge, the mixture should be solid. 6. For optimal enjoyment, cut into small pieces or squares. 7. If sealed properly, it has a week's worth of storage time in the fridge.

CREAMY ARTICHOKE DIP

Total Time: 15 minutes | Prep Time: 10 minutes

Ingredients:

1 can (14 oz) artichoke hearts, drained	1 cup cream cheese, softened
1/2 cup sour cream	1/2 cup grated Parmesan cheese
2 cloves garlic, minced	Salt and pepper to taste
Fresh parsley for garnish	

Directions:

1. The artichoke hearts, cream cheese, sour cream, Parmesan cheese, and garlic should be mixed together in the food processor that is manufactured by Cuisinart. 2. The mixture should be processed until it is silky, smooth, and creamy. 3. Salt and pepper should be added to taste, depending on the situation. 4. Place the dip in a dish that is fit for serving. 5. Mix in some fresh parsley as a garnish. 6. Use crackers, pita chips, or vegetables as accompaniments. 7. Seal any remaining food in an airtight container and store it in the fridge.

CINNAMON WALNUT BARS

Total Time: 40 minutes | Prep Time: 10 minutes

Ingredients:

1 cup walnuts	1 cup rolled oats
1/2 cup almond flour	1/2 cup maple syrup
1/2 teaspoon cinnamon	1/4 teaspoon salt

Directions:

1. Line an 8-by-8-inch baking dish with parchment. 2. Preheat the oven to 350°F. The walnuts, rolled oats, almond flour, cinnamon, and salt should be mixed together in the food processor that is a Cuisinart. Pulse until everything is well blended. 3. The maple syrup should be added, and the mixture should be pulsed until it comes together. 4. Create a uniform layer of the mixture in the prepared baking dish. 5. Bake for twenty to twenty-five minutes or until the top is golden brown. 6. Before cutting into bars, wait until the mixture has totally cooled. 7. For up to a week, store the mixture in a container that is airtight and at room temperature.

COCONUT MATCHA BARS

Total Time: 30 minutes | Prep Time: 10 minutes

Ingredients:

1 cup cashews	1 cup shredded unsweetened coconut
2 tablespoons matcha powder	1/2 cup maple syrup
1/4 teaspoon sea salt	

Directions:

1. Using parchment paper, line a baking dish that is 8 inches by 8 inches. 2. After combining cashews, shredded coconut, matcha powder, and sea salt in the Cuisinart food processor, proceed to process the mixture. Blend until the mixture is very fine. 3. After adding the maple syrup, continue processing the mixture until it becomes sticky and is well blended. 4. In the baking dish that has been prepared, press the mixture down firmly. 5. Place in the refrigerator for approximately twenty minutes or until the mixture has set. 6. Reduced to squares or bars in size. 7. You may keep it in the refrigerator for up to two weeks if you store it in an airtight container.

CASHEW BUTTER FUDGE BARS

Total Time: 25 minutes | Prep Time: 10 minutes

Ingredients:

1 cup cashew butter	1/4 cup honey or maple syrup
1/4 cup coconut oil, melted	1 teaspoon vanilla extract
1/2 cup chocolate chips (optional)	Pinch of salt

1. Use parchment paper to line an 8-by-8-inch baking dish. 2. Melt the coconut oil, add the cashew butter, honey or maple syrup, vanilla essence, and salt to the Cuisinart food processor. Puree the mixture. 3. Toss in the chocolate chips if you're using them. 4. After the baking dish is ready, pour in the ingredients and distribute it evenly. 5. To set, chill for approximately 15 minutes. 6. After it has hardened, cut it into bars. 7. Refrigerate for a maximum of two weeks if stored in an airtight container.

CARROT GINGER BALLS

Total Time: 30 minutes | Prep Time: 15 minutes

Ingredients:

2 cups grated carrots	1 cup rolled oats
1/2 cup almond flour	1/4 cup maple syrup
1 tablespoon fresh ginger, grated	1/2 teaspoon cinnamon
1/4 teaspoon nutmeg	Pinch of salt
1/2 cup shredded coconut (optional)	

Directions:

1. Put all of the ingredients into the Cuisinart Food Processor and pulse until smooth. Add the almond flour, maple syrup, ginger, cinnamon, nutmeg, and shredded carrots. Mix by pulsing. 2. You may add shredded coconut if you like, then pulse it one more to make sure it's properly distributed. 3. Gather the ingredients and shape them into balls, each approximately an inch in diameter. 4. Put the balls on a baking sheet that has been prepared with paper. 5. Set aside to firm up in the fridge for at least 15 minutes prior to serving. 6. Put any leftovers in a sealed container and store them in the fridge for no more than a week.

OATMEAL RAISIN BALLS

Total Time: 25 minutes | Prep Time: 10 minutes

Ingredients:

1 cup rolled oats	1/2 cup almond butter
1/2 cup honey or maple syrup	1/2 cup raisins
1 teaspoon cinnamon	1/4 teaspoon salt
1/4 cup chopped walnuts (optional)	

Directions:

1. In the Cuisinart Food Processor, combine the rolled oats, almond butter, honey (or maple syrup), raisins, cinnamon, and salt. Process until the ingredients are thoroughly combined. Mix well by pulsing the ingredients. 2. If using, add chopped walnuts and pulse a few times to incorporate them into the mixture. 3. To form balls, scoop the mixture and roll it into balls with a diameter of approximately one inch. 4. Carefully set the balls on top of a parchment-lined baking sheet. 5. Wait at least fifteen minutes in the refrigerator for the mixture to solidify. 6. It may be refrigerated for a week in an airtight jar with the ingredients.

FIG WALNUT SPREAD

Total Time: 10 minutes | Prep Time: 10 minutes

Ingredients:

1 cup dried figs, stems removed	1/2 cup walnuts
1 tablespoon lemon juice	1 teaspoon vanilla extract
Pinch of salt	

Directions:

1. Place the dried figs, walnuts, lemon juice, vanilla essence, and salt into the Cuisinart Food Processor and process until the mixture is smooth. 2. When necessary, scrape down the sides of the bowl as you process the mixture until it is completely smooth and well combined. 3. In order to obtain the required consistency, you may need to add a little bit of water or additional

lemon juice if the spread is too thick. 4. The dish should be transferred to a serving bowl and served with bread or crackers. 5. You may keep it in the refrigerator for up to two weeks if you store it in an airtight container.

CILANTRO LIME HUMMUS

Total Time: 15 minutes | Prep Time: 10 minutes

Ingredients:

1 can (15 oz) chickpeas	1/4 cup tahini
1/4 cup fresh lime juice	1/4 cup olive oil
1/2 cup fresh cilantro, packed	1 garlic clove
1/2 teaspoon cumin	Salt and pepper to taste

Directions:

1. Chickpeas, tahini, lime juice, olive oil, cilantro, garlic, and cumin should be mixed together in the Cuisinart Food Processor. 2. To get the required consistency, process until the mixture is completely smooth, adding water as necessary. 3. Depending on your preference, season with salt and pepper, and then mix one more to incorporate. 4. A sprinkle of more olive oil can be added to the hummus after it has been transferred to a serving dish. 5. It is recommended to serve with pita chips or fresh veggies. 6. It may be refrigerated for a week in an airtight jar with the ingredients.

RASPBERRY COCONUT BARS

Total Time: 40 minutes | Prep Time: 15 minutes

Ingredients:

1 cup rolled oats	1/2 cup almond flour
1/2 cup shredded coconut	1/4 cup honey or maple syrup
1 cup fresh or frozen raspberries	1/4 teaspoon salt

1/2 teaspoon vanilla extract

Directions:

1. Arrange parchment paper in an 8x8-inch baking dish and cook in an oven preheated to 175 degrees Celsius (350 degrees Fahrenheit). 2. Roll out the oats, add the almond flour and shredded coconut. Add the honey (or maple syrup), salt, and vanilla essence. Pulse until well combined. Mix by pulsing. 3. In a preheated baking dish, evenly distribute half of the mixture and press down firmly. 4. After pressing the mixture, evenly distribute the raspberries over it. Sprinkle the leftover oat mixture on top. 5. Brown the top of the dish after 25 minutes in the oven. 6. Let it cool entirely before slicing it into bars. Keep for up to a week in a sealed container.

PECAN PIE BARS

Total Time: 1 hour | Prep Time: 20 minutes

Ingredients:

1 cup all-purpose flour	1/2 cup unsalted butter, softened
1/4 cup brown sugar	1/2 teaspoon salt
1 cup pecans, chopped	1/2 cup corn syrup
1/2 cup granulated sugar	2 large eggs
1 teaspoon vanilla extract	

Directions:

1. Put the oven on high heat (350 degrees Fahrenheit, 175 degrees Celsius). 2. Pat down a baking pan that is 8 inches square. 3. Blend together the flour, butter, brown sugar, and salt in the food processor. Break into crumbles by pulsing in a food processor. 4. Put the crust together by pressing the ingredients into the bottom of the pan. After 15 minutes in the oven, remove from the oven. 5. Fluff up the eggs and vanilla with the corn syrup and granulated sugar in a basin. 6. After the crust has been pre-baked, pour the liquid over it and stir in the chopped

pecans. 7. To get a solid texture, bake for another 25 to 30 minutes. 8. After it has cooled, slice it into bars.

RED CURRY PASTE

Total Time: 15 minutes | Prep Time: 10 minutes

Ingredients:

2 tablespoons coriander seeds	1 tablespoon cumin seeds
1 teaspoon black peppercorns	1 tablespoon turmeric powder
2-3 dried red chilies	3-4 garlic cloves
1-2 lemongrass stalks, chopped	1-inch piece ginger, peeled and chopped
2 tablespoons vegetable oil	

Directions:

1. To bring out their fragrant scent, roast the cumin, coriander, and black peppercorns in a skillet over medium heat. 2. The spices should be allowed to cool slightly before being added to the food processor. 3. Incorporate dried chiles, garlic, ginger, lemongrass, and turmeric into the mixture. 4. In order to produce the appropriate consistency, blend the ingredients until a paste is formed, adding vegetable oil as necessary. 5. It is possible to preserve it in the refrigerator for up to a month if you store it in a container that is airtight.

HERB ROASTED GARLIC SPREAD

Total Time: 30 minutes | Prep Time: 10 minutes

Ingredients:

1 head of garlic	1/2 cup cream cheese, softened
1/4 cup sour cream	2 tablespoons fresh herbs (like parsley and chives), chopped

Salt and pepper to taste

Directions:

1. Bake until the oven reaches 400 degrees Fahrenheit (200 degrees Celsius). Remove the top of the garlic head by slicing it. 2. Before roasting the garlic for twenty to twenty-five minutes, wrap it in foil and cook it. 3. Garlic cloves that have been roasted should be squeezed into the food processor. 4. Pour in the cream cheese, sour cream, herbs, and season with salt and pepper. Blend until it is completely smooth. 5. If it is required, adjust the seasoning. 6. Accompany the dish with crackers or bread.

COCONUT PISTACHIO BALLS

Total Time: 20 minutes | Prep Time: 10 minutes

Ingredients:

1 cup pitted dates	1 cup unsweetened shredded coconut
1/2 cup raw pistachios	1/4 teaspoon salt
1 teaspoon vanilla extract	

Directions:

1. Put the dates, coconut, pistachios, salt, and vanilla extract into the food processor and begin processing. 2. To make the mixture sticky and to blend it, pulse it till it is. 3. Take a tiny amount of the contents and roll them into balls. 4. The balls can be rolled in more shredded coconut if that is what you want. 5. Before serving, place the mixture in the refrigerator for ten minutes to allow it to become more solid.

PEANUT BUTTER BANANA BALLS

Total Time: 15 minutes | Prep Time: 5 minutes

Ingredients:

1 ripe banana	1/2 cup peanut butter

1/2 cup oats

1/4 cup honey

1/2 teaspoon cinnamon

1/4 cup honey

1/2 cup dried cherries, chopped

1/4 cup almond slices

1 teaspoon vanilla extract

Directions:

1. Bananas, peanut butter, oats, honey, and cinnamon should be included in the food processor and mixed together. 2. Blend everything together until it's really smooth. 3. Take amounts that are about the size of a tablespoon and roll them into balls. 4. Collect the balls and arrange them in a single layer on a baking sheet that has been covered with parchment paper. 5. Keep in the refrigerator for half an hour to harden. 6. Put it in the refrigerator in a container that can seal out air.

CHIPOTLE LIME MAYO

Total Time: 10 minutes | Prep Time: 5 minutes

Ingredients:

1 cup mayonnaise

1-2 chipotle peppers in adobo sauce

1 tablespoon lime juice

1 teaspoon garlic powder

Salt to taste

Directions:

1. Mayonnaise, chipotle peppers, lime juice, and garlic powder should be mixed together in a food processor. 2. Puree till it is silky, smooth, and creamy. 3. Examine the flavor, and if required, adjust the seasoning with salt. 4. Before usage, place the mixture in a jar and place it in the refrigerator for at least half an hour. 5. Use it as a spread for sandwiches or as a dip.

CHERRY ALMOND ENERGY BITES

Total Time: 20 minutes | Prep Time: 10 minutes

Ingredients:

1 cup rolled oats

1/2 cup almond butter

Directions:

1. Put the almond butter, honey, oats, dried cherries, almond slices, and vanilla essence into the food processor. 2. Run the mixture through the blender until it becomes sticky. 3. Roll the mixture into balls using spoonfuls. 4. Layer the balls on a parchment-lined baking sheet. 5. Before serving, let it rest in the fridge for half an hour. 6. You may keep it in the fridge for up to a week if you seal it well.

CUCUMBER MINT YOGURT

Total Time: 10 minutes | Prep Time: 10 minutes

Ingredients:

1 cup Greek yogurt

1 cucumber, peeled and finely chopped

2 tablespoons fresh mint leaves, chopped

1 tablespoon lemon juice

Salt and pepper to taste

Directions:

1. Toss the Greek yogurt, cucumber, and mint leaves in the food processor bowl of your Cuisinart appliance. 2. The lemon juice should be squeezed in just before serving, and salt and pepper should be added as desired. 3. Blend or process until very creamy, stopping to scrape down edges as necessary. 4. Reevaluate the seasoning by tasting. 5. After transferring to a serving bowl, allow the flavors to combine by chilling for 30 minutes. 6. Use it as a sauce or dip with your favorite foods after it's cold.

GREEK YOGURT RANCH

Total Time: 10 minutes | Prep Time: 10 minutes

Ingredients:

1 cup Greek yogurt	1 tablespoon fresh dill, chopped
1 tablespoon fresh parsley, chopped	1 teaspoon garlic powder
1 teaspoon onion powder	1 tablespoon lemon juice
Salt and pepper to taste	

Directions:

1. Add the dill, parsley, garlic powder, onion powder, and lemon juice to the bowl of a Cuisinart Food Processor. Combine the Greek yogurt with the ingredients. 2. Salt and pepper should be added to taste, according to your preferences. 3. The mixture should be blended until it is smooth, pausing occasionally to scrape down the edges. 4. If needed, taste and make seasoning adjustments. 5. After transferring it to a serving plate, let it sit in the fridge for 30 minutes to let the flavors meld. 6. As a salad dressing or to accompany fresh veggies, serve.

CASHEW ALMOND BALLS

Total Time: 15 minutes | Prep Time: 15 minutes

Ingredients:

1 cup cashews	1 cup almonds
1 tablespoon honey	1 teaspoon vanilla extract
1/2 teaspoon salt	Optional: shredded coconut or chopped nuts for coating

Directions:

1. The cashews and almonds should be added to the Cuisinart food processor. Crush to a fine powder, but not powdery, consistency. 2. Honey, vanilla essence, and salt should be added. The mixture will begin to clump together after processing. 3. Just a touch of additional honey will fix a dry combination. 4. Make little balls out of the mixture, each approximately an inch in diameter. 5. To coat the balls, you may either roll them in shredded coconut or cut some nuts. 6. When you are finished, place the balls on a baking sheet and place them in the refrigerator for at least half an hour so that they can solidify. 7. Try it as a sweet treat or nutritious nibble.

HONEY MUSTARD DRESSING

Total Time: 5 minutes | Prep Time: 5 minutes

Ingredients:

1/4 cup honey	1/4 cup Dijon mustard
1/4 cup apple cider vinegar	1/2 cup olive oil
Salt and pepper to taste	

Directions:

1. Use the Cuisinart Food Processor to combine the honey, Dijon mustard, and apple cider vinegar. Blend everything together until smooth. 2. Gradually pour olive oil into the food processor while it operates to create an emulsified dressing. 3. Season with salt and pepper before grinding everything. 4. Take a taste, and if necessary, adjust the level of sweetness or acidity. 5. Before serving, place the mixture in a jar and place it in the refrigerator for at least half an hour. 6. After giving it a good shake, you can use it as a dip or as a topping for salads.

LEMON PARSLEY SAUCE

Total Time: 10 minutes | Prep Time: 10 minutes

Ingredients:

1/2 cup fresh parsley leaves	1/4 cup olive oil
1 tablespoon lemon juice	1 clove garlic
Salt and pepper to taste	

1. Place the parsley, olive oil, lemon juice, and garlic in the bowl of the Cuisinart Food Processor. Mix until everything is evenly distributed. 2. When necessary, scrape down the sides of the bowl as you process the mixture until it is completely smooth and well combined. 3. Add salt and pepper to taste. 4. Slightly additional olive oil or lemon juice can be used to thin down the sauce if it seems too thick. 5. Take a taste, and make any necessary adjustments to the seasoning. 6. It may be served right away, or it can be stored in the refrigerator for up to a week. 7. Serve this sauce on top of grilled meats or veggies for a delicious flavor.

CILANTRO LIME DRESSING

Total Time: 10 minutes | Prep Time: 10 minutes

Ingredients:

1 cup fresh cilantro leaves, packed	1/4 cup lime juice
1/4 cup olive oil	1 garlic clove, minced
1/2 teaspoon salt	1/4 teaspoon black pepper
1 teaspoon honey or agave syrup (optional)	

Directions:

1. Mix the cilantro, lime juice, garlic, salt, and black pepper in the Cuisinart food processor until everything is evenly distributed. 2. Pulse the cilantro until it is cut into very little pieces. 3. While the food processor is operating, gradually blend in the olive oil until it is completely incorporated. 4. Take a taste and make any necessary adjustments to the spice; if you like, you can also add honey or agave syrup. 5. Place in a jar, and store in the refrigerator until you are ready to use it. 6. Because the ingredients could separate, give it a good shake before serving.

ALMOND BUTTER

Total Time: 15 minutes | Prep Time: 15 minutes

Ingredients:

2 cups raw almonds	1/2 teaspoon salt (optional)
1-2 tablespoons honey or maple syrup (optional)	1 tablespoon oil (optional for creaminess)

Directions:

1. The Cuisinart food processor should be filled with unprocessed almonds. 2. Perform the processing at a high speed for approximately ten to twelve minutes, scraping down the edges as required. 3. Continue to grind the almonds until they transform into butter that is silky, smooth, and creamy. 4. If desired, add salt and sugar, and then pulse to blend the ingredients. 5. In the event that the almond butter is too thick, gradually incorporate oil into it, one tablespoon at a time, until you get the appropriate density. 6. In a clean jar, transfer the mixture, and then place it in the refrigerator.

INDIAN SPICED CHUTNEY

Total Time: 15 minutes | Prep Time: 15 minutes

Ingredients:

1 cup fresh cilantro leaves	1/2 cup fresh mint leaves
1-2 green chilies, chopped (to taste)	1 tablespoon ginger, grated
1 tablespoon lime juice	1 teaspoon cumin powder
Salt to taste	Water, as needed for consistency

Directions:

1. Put the cilantro, mint, green chilies, ginger, lime juice, and cumin powder into the Cuisinart food processor and mix them together before proceeding. 2. The herbs should be processed until they are finely chopped. 3. Combine the salt by pulsing it in there. 4. The chutney should be made by gradually adding water, one tablespoon at a time until it achieves the consistency you

wish. 5. Test the seasoning, then make any required adjustments. 6. Pour the mixture into a dish and use it as a dip or to accompany small bites.

CREAMY GUACAMOLE

Total Time: 10 minutes | Prep Time: 10 minutes

Ingredients:

2 ripe avocados	1/4 cup red onion, chopped
1 small tomato, diced	1 lime, juiced
1 clove garlic, minced	Salt to taste
Fresh cilantro, chopped (optional)	

Directions:

1. After removing the pit from the avocados, cut them in half lengthwise, and then scoop the flesh into the Cuisinart food processor. 2. With garlic, lime juice, and salt, pulse the mixture until smooth or to your desired consistency. 3. To incorporate the red onion and tomato, pulse the food processor a few times without completely blending them. 4. If you want to add some more flavor, you may fold in some chopped cilantro. 5. Transfer the mixture to a dish for serving, and if wanted, garnish it with extra crushed cilantro. 6. Immediately serve with tortilla chips or fresh veggies after preparation.

GINGER COCONUT BALLS

Total Time: 20 minutes | Prep Time: 20 minutes

Ingredients:

1 cup unsweetened shredded coconut	1/2 cup almond flour
1/4 cup maple syrup or honey	1 tablespoon fresh ginger, grated
1 teaspoon vanilla extract	Pinch of salt

Directions:

1. Put the shredded coconut, almond flour, maple syrup, grated ginger, vanilla essence, and salt into the Cuisinart food processor. Process until everything is nicely combined. 2. The mixture should be processed until it is completely mixed and sticky. 3. Scoop out amounts that are about the size of a tablespoon and shape them into balls. 4. Line a tray with parchment paper and place the balls on it. 5. Allow it to chill in the refrigerator for at least half an hour to set. 6. You may keep it in the refrigerator for up to a week if you store it in an airtight container.

APPLE CINNAMON BALLS

Total Time: 30 minutes | Prep Time: 15 minutes

Ingredients:

2 cups rolled oats	1 cup unsweetened applesauce
1/2 cup almond butter	1/4 cup honey or maple syrup
1 teaspoon cinnamon	1/4 teaspoon salt
1/2 cup chopped walnuts	

Directions:

1. The rolled oats, applesauce, almond butter, honey, cinnamon, and salt should be mixed together in the Cuisinart Food Processor prior to processing. Pulse until everything is well combined. 2. To combine chopped nuts, pulse a few times. 3. The dough should be formed into little balls with a diameter of around one inch using either your hands or a cookie scoop. 4. Gather the balls and set them on a parchment-lined baking sheet. 5. Chill for around fifteen minutes in order to firm up. 6. Either consume it right away or put it in a container that seals well and put it in the refrigerator for up to a week.

PESTO ROSSO

Total Time: 15 minutes | Prep Time: 10 minutes

Ingredients:

1 cup sun-dried tomatoes

1/2 cup fresh basil leaves

1/4 cup pine nuts

1/4 cup grated Parmesan cheese

2 cloves garlic

1/4 cup olive oil

Salt and pepper to taste

Directions:

1. Sun-dried tomatoes, basil, pine nuts, Parmesan cheese, and garlic should be mixed together in the Cuisinart Food Processor. Pulse until the mixture is coarsely minced. 2. Olive oil should be added in a slow and steady stream while the engine is running until the mixture is completely smooth. 3. Make sure to stop and scrape down the edges of the bowl whenever necessary. 4. After pulsing the ingredients together, season them with salt and pepper to taste. 5. At the time of serving, the mixture should be transferred to a bowl and served immediately. Alternatively, you may preserve it in the refrigerator for up to a week in an airtight container.

ALMOND PESTO

Total Time: 10 minutes | Prep Time: 5 minutes

Ingredients:

2 cups fresh basil leaves

1/2 cup almonds (raw or roasted)

1/4 cup grated Parmesan cheese

2 cloves garlic

1/4 cup olive oil

Salt and pepper to taste

Directions:

1. Basil leaves, almonds, Parmesan cheese, and garlic should be mixed together in the Cuisinart Food Processor. Pulse until the mixture is roughly chopped. 2. While processing, drizzle in the olive oil little by little until the pesto has the consistency you like. 3. When it is required, pause the process and scrape down the edges of

the bowl. 4. After pulsing the ingredients once again, season them with salt and pepper to taste. 5. Immediately serve with pasta or bread or as a dip, or keep it in the refrigerator in an airtight container. In addition, serve immediately.

CARAMEL CASHEW BALLS

Total Time: 20 minutes | Prep Time: 10 minutes

Ingredients:

1 cup pitted dates

1 cup raw cashews

1/4 cup almond butter

1 teaspoon vanilla extract

1/4 teaspoon sea salt

1/4 cup shredded coconut (optional)

Directions:

1. Put the cashews, dates, almond butter, vanilla essence, and salt into the Cuisinart food processor. Mix everything together until it becomes sticky, then pulse. 2. Pulse the ingredients once more after adding a tablespoon of water if they seem too dry. 3. Gather the ingredients and shape them into little balls, each approximately 1 inch in diameter. 4. For an optional coating, you may roll the balls in shredded coconut. 5. Set the balls aside to harden up in the fridge for at least 10 minutes after placing them on a platter. 6. Take it with you or put it in the fridge for up to a week in an airtight container.

MAPLE PECAN BITES

Total Time: 15 minutes | Prep Time: 10 minutes

Ingredients:

1 cup pecans

1 cup pitted dates

1/4 cup maple syrup

1 teaspoon vanilla extract

1/4 teaspoon cinnamon

Pinch of salt

Directions:

1. A mixture of pecans and dates should be processed in the Cuisinart Food Processor. Pulse

until the ingredients are blended and coarsely minced. 2. Vanilla essence, cinnamon, and salt should be added along with maple syrup. Repeat the pulsing process until evenly combined. 3. Remove the mixture from the bowl and use your hands to shape it into bite-sized balls or bite-sized pieces. 4. Bake the parts once you've lined a baking sheet with parchment paper. 5. Keep in the refrigerator for ten to fifteen minutes to harden. 6. You may consume it right once, or you can take it to the refrigerator and preserve it in an airtight container for up to a week.

SILKY BUTTERNUT SQUASH SOUP

Total Time: 30 minutes | Prep Time: 10 minutes

Ingredients:

1 medium butternut squash, peeled and cubed	1 onion, chopped
2 cloves garlic, minced	4 cups vegetable or chicken broth
1 tsp ground ginger	1 tsp cinnamon
Salt and pepper to taste	1 cup coconut milk (optional)
Olive oil for sautéing	

Directions:

1. Chop the garlic and onion finely in a Cuisinart food processor. 2. Put the olive oil in a saucepan and set it over medium heat. After three to five minutes of sautéing, the garlic and onion mixture should be transparent. 3. Spice it up with some salt, pepper, ginger, cinnamon, and diced butternut squash. Coat well to blend. 4. Before adding the chicken or veggies, bring the liquid to a boil. After the squash has begun to soften, reduce the heat and simmer for another ten to fifteen minutes. 5. To get a smooth puree, purée the soup in batches in the food processor. 6. If using coconut milk, whisk it into the soup before returning it to the saucepan and heating it through. 7. Warm it up and top it with cinnamon if you want.

WALNUT CARROT SPREAD

Total Time: 15 minutes | Prep Time: 10 minutes

Ingredients:

2 cups grated carrots	1 cup walnuts, toasted
2 tablespoons olive oil	1 tablespoon lemon juice
1 clove garlic	Salt and pepper to taste
Fresh herbs (like parsley or dill)	

Directions:

1. Carrots that have been grated, walnuts that have been roasted, olive oil, lemon juice, garlic, salt, and pepper should be added to the Cuisinart Food Processor. 2. While pulsing, the mixture should be thoroughly blended but should still have some chunks. 3. Take a taste, and make any necessary adjustments to the seasoning. 4. Transfer the spread to a bowl that is intended for serving, and then top it with fresh herbs. 5. This meal goes well with crackers, bread, or veggies as a dip.

CREAMY HERB DIP

Total Time: 10 minutes | Prep Time: 5 minutes

Ingredients:

1 cup Greek yogurt	1/2 cup sour cream
1 tablespoon lemon juice	2 tablespoons fresh dill, chopped
1 tablespoon fresh parsley, chopped	1 clove garlic, minced
Salt and pepper to taste	

Directions:

1. Put the Greek yogurt, sour cream, lemon juice, dill, parsley, and garlic into the Cuisinart Food Processor and mix them together well. 2. Mix the herbs in a food processor until they are finely

minced, and the dip is smooth. 3. After you taste it and season it with salt and pepper, pulse it again to mix the ingredients. 4. Place the dip in a dish that is fit for serving. 5. In order to allow the flavors to combine, chill the dish for at least half an hour before serving. 6. Aside from pita chips and fresh vegetables, this recipe is also delicious spread over sandwiches.

VANILLA PROTEIN BALLS

Total Time: 15 minutes | Prep Time: 10 minutes

Ingredients:

1 cup rolled oats	1/2 cup almond butte
1/4 cup honey or maple syrup	1/4 cup vanilla protein powder
1/4 cup mini chocolate chips (optional)	1 teaspoon vanilla extract
A pinch of salt	

Directions:

1. Add the oats, almond butter, honey, protein powder, vanilla extract, and salt to the Cuisinart Food Processor and mix until everything is combined. 2. Perform a series of pulses until the mixture is thoroughly mixed and adheres to itself. Add a little water or additional nut butter if the mixture is too dry. 3. If you are using tiny chocolate chips, stir them in. 4. Form the mixture into balls by scooping out sections of it that are about the size of a tablespoon. 5. Position the balls onto a parchment paper-lined baking sheet. 6. Allow it to chill in the refrigerator for at least half an hour to set. 7. With proper airtight storage, this may be chilled for up to seven days.

PECAN ALMOND BALLS

Total Time: 30 minutes | Prep Time: 15 minutes

Ingredients:

1 cup pecans	1 cup almonds
1 cup dates, pitted	1 tsp vanilla extract

½ tsp cinnamon ¼ tsp sea salt

Unsweetened shredded coconut for rolling (optional)

Directions:

1. Chop the almonds and pecans coarsely in a Cuisinart food processor, but don't smash them. 2. Toss the nuts with the dates, vanilla essence, cinnamon, and sea salt. To make a sticky mixture, process until all ingredients are well incorporated. 3. Make little balls out of the mixture, each approximately an inch in diameter. 4. Coat the balls completely with crushed coconut if you like. 5. To solidify balls, chill them on a parchment-lined baking sheet for 15 minutes. 6. Refrigerate for up to seven days if stored in an airtight container. 7. Indulge in this guilt-free sweet treat!

SPICED CHAI BITES

Total Time: 25 minutes | Prep Time: 10 minutes

Ingredients:

1 cup rolled oats	½ cup almond butter
½ cup honey or maple syrup	1 tsp chai spice mix (or ½ tsp cinnamon, ½ tsp ginger, ¼ tsp cardamom)
1 tsp vanilla extract	¼ cup chocolate chips (optional)

Directions:

1. Gather the rolled oats, almond butter, honey or maple syrup, chai spice mix, and vanilla essence in a Cuisinart food processor. 2. Blend or process until the ingredients are thoroughly incorporated, and the result resembles dough. 3. Use a spatula to gently incorporate the chocolate chips, if using. 4. Form little balls out of the mixture, about an inch in diameter. 5. After placing the bits on a parchment-lined baking sheet, lay them aside in the fridge for 15 minutes. 6. Refrigerate for up to seven days if stored in an

airtight container. 7. Snack on them for a healthy treat!

SWEET POTATO MASH

Total Time: 30 minutes | Prep Time: 10 minutes

Ingredients:

2 large sweet potatoes, peeled and cubed	2 tbsp butter or olive oil
¼ cup milk (or non-dairy alternative)	½ tsp cinnamon
Salt and pepper to taste	

Directions:

1. After placing the sweet potatoes in cubes, fill them with water and place them in a big saucepan. Cook until soft, which should take around 15–20 minutes, after bringing to a boil. 2. After draining the sweet potatoes, place them in the food processor that is manufactured by Cuisinart. 3. Cinnamon, salt, pepper, and butter or olive oil should be added to the mixture. 4. Process until the mixture is silky smooth and creamy, scraping down the sides as necessary. 5. The seasoning should be tasted and adjusted as required. 6. To serve as a side dish, serve warm. 7. I hope you like your mash made with sweet potatoes!

TROPICAL COCONUT BALLS

Total Time: 20 minutes | Prep Time: 10 minutes

Ingredients:

1 cup dried mango, chopped	1 cup unsweetened shredded coconut
1 cup almonds	½ cup cashew butter
1 tsp vanilla extract	

Directions:

1. Prepare the almonds by pulsing them in a Cuisinart food processor until they are finely chopped. 2. The cashew butter, shredded coconut, dried mango, and vanilla essence should all be added to the food processor. 3. Be sure to process the mixture until it becomes sticky and thoroughly uniform. 4. Through the use of your hands, shape the mixture into little balls with a diameter of approximately one inch. 5. To solidify, freeze the balls on a parchment-lined baking sheet for 10 minutes. 6. You may keep it in the refrigerator for up to a week if you store it in an airtight container. 7. Have it as a dessert or a snack for a refreshing tropical experience!

CHOCOLATE HAZELNUT BITES

Total Time: 30 minutes | Prep Time: 15 minutes

Ingredients:

1 cup raw hazelnuts	1 cup Medjool dates, pitted
1/2 cup dark chocolate chips	1 tablespoon cocoa powder
1 teaspoon vanilla extract	Pinch of salt

Directions:

1. Start the oven to 350 degrees Fahrenheit (175 degrees Celsius) for baking. In a baking pan, roast the hazelnuts for approximately 10 minutes or until they release their aroma. 2. The Cuisinart Food Processor needs the hazelnuts to chill a little before processing. 3. Coarsely chop the nuts (do not purée) in a food processor. 4. Process the dates with the cocoa powder, salt, vanilla essence, and dates. Blend or process until a sticky consistency is achieved. 5. Gather parchment paper and set it aside. Place inch-diameter dough balls on the baking sheet. 6. After melting the dark chocolate chips, dip each ball and place it on the parchment paper. You may use a microwave or double boiler to achieve this. 7. To set, chill the bits coated in chocolate for approximately 15 minutes. 8. You may keep it in the fridge for up to a week if you seal it well.

DARK CHOCOLATE CHERRY BALLS

Total Time: 25 minutes | Prep Time: 10 minutes

Ingredients:

1 cup dried cherries	1 cup almonds
1/2 cup dark chocolate chips	1 tablespoon honey or maple syrup
1/4 cup unsweetened cocoa powder	1/2 teaspoon vanilla extract

Directions:

1. Chop the almonds and dried cherries in a Cuisinart food processor. Mix and process until the ingredients are coarsely chopped. 2. Combine the dark chocolate chips, vanilla essence, cocoa powder, honey (or maple syrup), and honey. Blend or process until a sticky consistency is achieved. 3. Tiny balls (about 1 inch in diameter) are formed by scooping out portions of the mixture. 4. On a baking sheet lined with paper, arrange the balls. 5. As an optional finishing touch, roll each ball in more chocolate powder. 6. To set, chill for approximately 15 minutes. 7. Keep in the fridge for up to a week if sealed tightly.

MAPLE PECAN ENERGY BITES

Total Time: 20 minutes | Prep Time: 10 minutes

Ingredients:

1 cup pecans	1 cup rolled oats
1/2 cup almond butter	1/4 cup maple syrup
1/4 teaspoon cinnamon	Pinch of salt

Directions:

1. In a Cuisinart food processor, pulse the pecans until they are finely chopped. 2. Toss in the almond butter, maple syrup, rolled oats, cinnamon, and salt. To make a sticky mixture, process until all ingredients are well incorporated. 3. Make 1-inch, bite-sized balls from the mixture. 4. Place energy bites on parchment-lined baking sheets. 5. Set aside in the fridge for approximately 10 minutes. 6. There

is no need to wait to savor it; it can stay in the fridge for up to a week if sealed properly. 7. You may store them in the freezer for even longer.

LEMON ZEST BALLS

Total Time: 20 minutes | Prep Time: 10 minutes

Ingredients:

1 cup raw cashews	1 cup Medjool dates, pitted
Zest of 1 lemon	1 tablespoon lemon juice
1/2 teaspoon vanilla extract	Pinch of salt

Directions:

1. Pulse the cashews finely in the Cuisinart Food Processor to get them finely chopped. 2. Combine the Medjool dates with the salt, lemon zest, lemon juice, and vanilla essence. The mixture will get sticky after processing. 3. Tiny balls (about 1 inch in diameter) are formed by scooping out portions of the mixture. 4. On a baking sheet lined with paper, arrange the balls. 5. Not required: To add texture and taste, roll the balls in shredded coconut. 6. Put in the fridge for approximately 10 minutes to set. 7. Keep in the fridge for up to a week if sealed tightly.

CHAI SPICED ALMOND BARS

Total Time: 45 minutes | Prep Time: 15 minutes

Ingredients:

1 1/2 cups almonds	1 cup Medjool dates, pitted
2 tablespoons chia seeds	1 teaspoon ground cinnamon
1/2 teaspoon ground ginger	1/4 teaspoon ground cardamom
Pinch of salt	

Directions:

1. The oven should be preheated to 350°F or 175°C. Ensure that the bottom of a baking dish is

covered with parchment paper. 2. Toss the almonds into the Cuisinart Food Processor and process until they are finely minced. 3. Incorporate the salt, cinnamon, ginger, chia seeds, Medjool dates, and cardamom. Blend or process until a sticky consistency is achieved. 4. Spread the ingredients out evenly in the baking dish that has been prepared. 5. Cook for approximately 20 minutes, and then allow it to cool within the pan. 6. After it has cooled, slice it into squares or bars. 7. You may keep it for up to a week in an airtight jar at room temperature.

MAPLE ALMOND BARS

Total Time: 2 hours | Prep Time: 30 minutes

Ingredients:

1 cup almond flour	1 cup rolled oats
1/2 cup maple syrup	1/4 cup almond butter
1/2 teaspoon vanilla extract	1/4 teaspoon salt
1/4 cup chopped almonds (for topping)	

Directions:

1. Mixed together in a Cuisinart food processor are the following Ingredients: almond flour, rolled oats, maple syrup, almond butter, salt, and vanilla extract. Blend the ingredients together by pulsing the mixture. 2. Use parchment paper to line an 8-by-8-inch baking dish. Distribute the mixture evenly on the base of the casserole. 3. Before gently pressing them into the mixture, sprinkle the chopped almonds on top. 4. Put in the fridge for at least an hour or until it sets. 5. Cut into bars after removing from baking dish. 6. Let it sit in the fridge for at least a few hours before using.

CHOCOLATE CHERRY BARS

Total Time: 1 hour 30 minutes | Prep Time: 20 minutes

Ingredients:

1 cup pitted dates	1/2 cup dried cherries
1/2 cup almonds	1/4 cup cocoa powder
1/2 teaspoon vanilla extract	1/4 teaspoon salt
1/4 cup dark chocolate chips (optional)	

Directions:

1. Process dates, almonds, dried cherries, cocoa powder, vanilla essence, and salt. Mix until a sticky dough is formed. 2. Use parchment paper to line an 8-by-8-inch baking dish. Firmly press the mixture into the dish's base. 3. Toss in some dark chocolate chips and mash them lightly into the mixture if you want. 4. Take the dish out of the refrigerator and let it rest there for at least an hour. 5. Take it out of the pan and cut it into bars when it's set. 6. Let it sit in the fridge for at least a few hours before using.

PISTACHIO COCONUT BALLS

Total Time: 45 minutes | Prep Time: 15 minutes

Ingredients:

1 cup unsweetened shredded coconut	1 cup pistachios (shelled)
1/4 cup maple syrup	1/2 teaspoon vanilla extract

Pinch of salt

Directions:

1. The pistachios should be pulsed in the food processor until they are finely chopped down. Make sure that you do not overprocess the mixture into a paste. 2. Put the shredded coconut, maple syrup, vanilla essence, and salt into the food processor. Process until just combined. Pulse until everything is well blended. 3. Form the mixture into balls by scooping out sections of it that are about the size of a tablespoon. 4. For

30 minutes, refrigerate the balls on a prepared baking sheet to firm up. 5. Ensure that the container is sealed and place it in the refrigerator.

PUMPKIN WALNUT BALLS

Total Time: 1 hour | Prep Time: 20 minutes

Ingredients:

1 cup pumpkin puree	1 cup walnuts
1/4 cup maple syrup	1 teaspoon cinnamon
1/2 teaspoon nutmeg	1/4 teaspoon salt
1/4 cup rolled oats (optional for texture)	

Directions:

1. Mix pumpkin puree, walnuts, maple syrup, cinnamon, nutmeg, and salt in a food processor. Maintain a smooth consistency. 2. If using rolled oats, pulse them into the mixture. 3. Take amounts that are about the size of a tablespoon and roll them into balls. 4. Once the balls have been arranged on a baking sheet that has been prepared, place them in the refrigerator for approximately half an hour. 5. Ensure that the container is sealed and place it in the refrigerator.

PECAN PIE BALLS

Total Time: 1 hour | Prep Time: 20 minutes

Ingredients:

1 cup pecans	1/2 cup pitted dates
1/4 cup maple syrup	1 teaspoon vanilla extract
1/4 teaspoon salt	

Directions:

1. Pulse pecans in a food processor until roughly chopped. 2. Put in some salt, maple syrup, vanilla essence, and dates that have been pitted. Be sure to process the mixture until it becomes sticky and thoroughly uniform. 3. Take amounts that are about the size of a tablespoon and roll them

into balls. 4. Refrigerate the balls for 30 minutes after placing them on a preheated baking sheet to solidify. 5. Ensure that the container is sealed and place it in the refrigerator.

FRESH LEMON VINAIGRETTE

Total Time: 10 minutes | Prep Time: 10 minutes

Ingredients:

1/4 cup fresh lemon juice	1/2 cup olive oil
1 teaspoon Dijon mustard	1 teaspoon honey
Salt and pepper to taste	

Directions:

1. Honey, lemon juice, and Dijon mustard should be mixed together in the food processor bowl. 2. Just a few pulses will be enough to combine the ingredients. 3. Keep slowly adding olive oil to the food processor until the dressing is well emulsified. 4. In addition to seasoning with salt, add pepper and salt to taste. 5. After transferring the mixture to a dish or jar, place it in the refrigerator until you are ready to use it.

TZATZIKI SAUCE

Total Time: 15 minutes | Prep Time: 15 minutes

Ingredients:

1 cup Greek yogurt	1/2 cucumber, peeled and grated
2 cloves garlic, minced	1 tablespoon olive oil
1 tablespoon fresh dill, chopped	1 tablespoon lemon juice
Salt to taste	

Directions:

1. Put the shredded cucumber in the food processor and give it a few pulses to get rid of any extra moisture. 2. In a bowl, combine the following Ingredients: Greek yogurt, garlic, olive

oil, dill, lemon juice, and salt. 3. Continue mixing until everything is creamy. 4. Test the seasoning, then make any required adjustments. 5. Place in a bowl suitable for serving and place in the refrigerator for at least half an hour to let the flavors combine.

MATCHA PISTACHIO BALLS

Total Time: 20 minutes | Prep Time: 20 minutes

Ingredients:

1 cup pitted Medjool dates	1 cup raw pistachios
1 tablespoon matcha powder	1/4 cup almond flour
Pinch of salt	1 teaspoon vanilla extract

Directions:

1. Place the dates that have been pitted into the food processor and pulse them until they create a sticky paste. 2. Pistachios in their raw form, matcha powder, almond flour, salt, and vanilla essence should be added now. 3. Repeat the process until the ingredients are well incorporated and a dough is formed. 4. The mixture should be rolled into little balls with a diameter of approximately one inch. 5. Refrigerate the balls for at least half an hour before serving them. Place them on a dish that has been lined with parchment paper.

CHERRY PECAN BARS

Total Time: 45 minutes | Prep Time: 15 minutes

Ingredients:

1 cup pitted dried cherries	1 cup pecans
1/2 cup almond flour	1/4 cup maple syrup
1 teaspoon vanilla extract	1/4 teaspoon salt
1/4 teaspoon cinnamon	

Directions:

1. To begin, use parchment paper to line a baking sheet measuring 8 inches by 8 inches, and next, bring the temperature of the oven up to 350 degrees Fahrenheit. 2. Combine the pecans and dried cherries in the food processor and mix until smooth. Pulse until extremely finely minced. 3. Put in some cinnamon, salt, and vanilla essence, along with some almond flour and maple syrup. Continue processing until a gooey mixture is formed. 4. Create a uniform layer of the mixture that has been prepared in the baking pan. 5. Cook for twenty to twenty-five minutes or until the edges are golden brown. When ready, cut into bars after allowing to cool.

CAULIFLOWER RICE PILAF

Total Time: 25 minutes | Prep Time: 10 minutes

Ingredients:

1 medium cauliflower, cut into florets	1 tablespoon olive oil
1 small onion, diced	2 cloves garlic, minced
1 cup vegetable broth	1/2 cup peas (fresh or frozen)
Salt and pepper to taste	Fresh parsley for garnish (optional)

Directions:

1. The cauliflower florets should be processed in the food processor until they have the appearance of rice grains. 2. Prepare the olive oil by heating it in a large pan over medium heat. Sauté the onion and garlic until they have become more tame. 3. Put the cauliflower rice in the pan and cook it for three to four minutes while stirring it occasionally. 4. It is then time to add the peas and pour in the vegetable broth. It should take around five to seven minutes for the beverage to be absorbed. 5. Before serving, sprinkle with fresh parsley and salt & pepper.

LEMON GINGER BALLS

Total Time: 20 minutes | Prep Time: 10 minutes

Ingredients:

1 cup almonds	1 cup dates, pitted
2 tablespoons fresh ginger, grated	1 tablespoon lemon juice
Zest of 1 lemon	1/4 teaspoon salt
Shredded coconut (for rolling)	

Directions:

1. Prepare the almonds by pulsing them in the food processor until they are finely chopped. 2. Add the dates that have been pitted, ginger that has been grated, lemon juice, lemon zest, and salt. Process the ingredients until they become sticky and are completely blended. 3. To make the balls, scoop out little amounts and roll them all together. 4. In order to provide a uniform coating, roll the balls in shredded coconut. 5. The lemon ginger balls should be placed on a dish and then placed in the refrigerator for ten minutes before being served. 6. You may keep it in the refrigerator for up to a week if you store it in an airtight container.

LEMON GARLIC SAUCE

Total Time: 10 minutes | Prep Time: 5 minutes

Ingredients:

1/2 cup olive oil	1/4 cup fresh lemon juice
4 cloves garlic, minced	1 teaspoon Dijon mustard
Salt and pepper to taste	Fresh herbs (optional, for garnish)

Directions:

1. Mix minced garlic, lemon juice, olive oil, and Dijon mustard in a food processor. 2. Process until the ingredients are thoroughly combined. 3. If necessary, alter the amount of salt and pepper that you use to season the dish. 4. In order to blend the fresh herbs, add them and pulse the food processor a few times. 5. After transferring it to a serving plate, allow it to sit for five minutes so that the flavors may combine. 6. Either as a dip or as a drizzle over veggies that have been roasted.

ROASTED TOMATO SAUCE

Total Time: 1 hour 10 minutes | Prep Time: 10 minutes

Ingredients:

2 pounds tomatoes, halved	1 onion, quartered
4 cloves garlic, unpeeled	2 tablespoons olive oil
Salt and pepper to taste	Fresh basil (for garnish)

Directions:

1. At 400 degrees Fahrenheit (200 degrees Celsius), preheat the oven. 2. Garlic, tomatoes, and onion should be arranged in a single layer on a baking sheet. 3. The dish should be seasoned with salt and pepper and then drizzled with olive oil. To get a uniform coating, toss the ingredients. 4. Roast the tomatoes in the oven for forty-five minutes or until they are tender and have a tiny layer of caramelization. 5. Wait until the garlic cloves have somewhat cooled down before peeling them. 6. Place the veggies that have been roasted in the food processor and process them until they are homogenous. 7. Test the seasoning, then make any required adjustments. Serve while still warm, with fresh basil as a garnish.

ORANGE HAZELNUT BARS

Total Time: 30 minutes | Prep Time: 15 minutes

Ingredients:

1 cup hazelnuts	1 cup pitted dates
1/2 cup rolled oats	Zest of 1 orange
1/4 cup fresh orange juice	1/4 teaspoon salt

Directions:

1. Preheat oven to 350°F. 2. Line a baking dish measuring 8 inches by 8 inches with parchment paper. 3. Pulse the hazelnuts in the food processor until they are finely ground. 4. Salt, citrus zest, rolled oats, and dates should be added to the mixture. Process until the ingredients are mixed and sticky. 5. The mixture should be pressed into the baking dish that has been prepared uniformly. 6. Bake for fifteen to twenty minutes or until beginning to turn brown. 7. Cut the mixture into bars only after it has cooled fully.

CHAI SPICE BALLS

Total Time: 20 minutes | Prep Time: 10 minutes

Ingredients:

1 cup rolled oats	1/2 cup almond butter
1/4 cup honey or maple syrup	2 teaspoons chai spice blend
1/4 cup raisins or dried cranberries	Pinch of salt

Directions:

1. Put the rolled oats, almond butter, honey (or maple syrup), chai spice blend, and process salt in the food processor until mixed. 2. The ingredients should be processed until they are thoroughly incorporated, and then a sticky dough should be formed. 3. To mix the ingredients, add the raisins or dried cranberries and whisk them in. 4. To make the balls, scoop out little amounts and roll them all together. 5. Put the balls on a dish and put them in the refrigerator for ten minutes so that they may harden. 6. You may keep it in the refrigerator for up to a week if you store it in an airtight container.

COCONUT CASHEW BALLS

Total Time: 20 minutes | Prep Time: 20 minutes

Ingredients:

1 cup cashews	1 cup unsweetened shredded coconut
1/4 cup honey or maple syrup	1 teaspoon vanilla extract
A pinch of salt	

Directions:

1. Cashews, shredded coconut, honey, vanilla essence, and salt should be mixed together in the food processor used by Cuisinart. 2. Pulse the ingredients until they are finely minced, and the mixture starts to clump down. 3. Take bits of the mixture that are about the size of a tablespoon, roll them, and shape them into balls. 4. Put the balls on a baking sheet that has been lined with parchment paper. 5. Put in the refrigerator for at least half an hour to allow it to become more solid before serving. 6. It may be refrigerated for a week in an airtight jar with the ingredients.

COCONUT CASHEW BARS

Total Time: 30 minutes | Prep Time: 20 minutes

Ingredients:

1 cup cashews	1 cup unsweetened shredded coconut
1/2 cup almond flour	1/4 cup honey or maple syrup
1/2 teaspoon vanilla extract	A pinch of salt

Directions:

1. Using parchment paper, line a baking dish that is 8 inches by 8 inches. 2. Mix cashews, shredded coconut, almond flour, honey, vanilla essence, and salt in a food processor. 3. The mixture should be well mixed and sticky after being pulsed. 4. In order to create a uniform layer, press the mixture firmly into the baking dish that has been prepared. 5. Set in the refrigerator for approximately ten minutes. 6. Once it has reached the desired consistency, cut it into bars

and place them in an airtight container in the refrigerator.

ALMOND LEMON BALLS

Total Time: 20 minutes | Prep Time: 20 minutes

Ingredients:

1 cup almonds	1 cup unsweetened shredded coconut
Zest of 1 lemon	1/4 cup honey or maple syrup
1 teaspoon lemon juice	A pinch of salt

Directions:

1. In a food processor from Cuisinart, add the following Ingredients: shredded coconut, almonds, lemon zest, honey, lemon juice, and cinnamon. 2. The mixture should be well combined and coarsely chopped. 3. Scoop out amounts that are about the size of a tablespoon and shape them into balls. 4. Line a tray with parchment paper and place the balls on it. 5. Allow it to chill in the refrigerator for at least half an hour to set. 6. This may be refrigerated for a week in an airtight container.

GINGER COCONUT BARS

Total Time: 30 minutes | Prep Time: 20 minutes

Ingredients:

1 cup unsweetened shredded coconut	1/2 cup almonds
1/4 cup honey or maple syrup	1 teaspoon ground ginger
1/2 teaspoon vanilla extract	A pinch of salt

Directions:

1. Line a baking dish measuring 8 inches by 8 inches with parchment paper. 2. Coconut shreds, almonds, honey, crushed ginger, vanilla essence, and salt should be mixed together in a food processor. 3. Proceed with the processing until the mixture is completely incorporated and sticky. 4. Create a uniform layer of the mixture by pressing it firmly into the baking dish that has been prepared. 5. To allow the mixture to harden, place it in the refrigerator for approximately ten minutes. 6. It should be cut into bars and then stored in an airtight refrigerator container.

TROPICAL COCONUT BARS

Total Time: 30 minutes | Prep Time: 20 minutes

Ingredients:

1 cup unsweetened shredded coconut	1/2 cup cashews
1/4 cup dried pineapple, chopped	1/4 cup honey or maple syrup
1/2 teaspoon vanilla extract	A pinch of salt

Directions:

1. Using parchment paper, line a baking dish that is 8 inches by 8 inches. 2. Put the shredded coconut, cashews, dried pineapple, honey, vanilla essence, and salt into the Cuisinart food processor. Process until everything is nicely combined. 3. Pulse the ingredients together until they are finely minced and sticky. 4. The mixture should be pressed into the baking dish that has been prepared in a uniform layer. 5. Set in the refrigerator for approximately ten minutes. 6. Cut into bars and place in a jar that is sealed and stored in the refrigerator.

ROASTED RED PEPPER HUMMUS

Total Time: 15 minutes | Prep Time: 10 minutes

Ingredients:

1 can (15 oz) chickpeas	1 cup roasted red peppers
2 tablespoons tahini	2 tablespoons lemon juice
2 cloves garlic, minced	2 tablespoons olive oil

1/2 teaspoon ground cumin

Salt and pepper to taste

Water (as needed for consistency)

Directions:

1. To make the chickpeas, roasted red peppers, tahini, lemon juice, garlic, olive oil, and cumin mixture, put all of the ingredients in the Cuisinart Food Processor. 2. The mixture should be processed until it is smooth, with the sides being scraped down as required. 3. If you find that the hummus is too thick, you may thin it down by adding water, one tablespoon at a time, until you achieve the consistency you want. 4. After seasoning with salt and pepper, pulse the ingredients for a few seconds. 5. Move the mixture to a bowl designed for serving, and before serving, sprinkle it with olive oil. In the event that you so wish, garnish with more roasted red peppers or parsley.

HERB AND GARLIC DIP

Total Time: 10 minutes | Prep Time: 5 minutes

Ingredients:

1 cup Greek yogurt	1/2 cup sour cream
2 cloves garlic, minced	1/4 cup fresh parsley, chopped
2 tablespoons fresh dill, chopped	1 tablespoon fresh chives, chopped
1 tablespoon lemon juice	Salt and pepper to taste

Directions:

1. Greek yogurt and sour cream should be mixed together in the Cuisinart Food Processor. 2. Garlic that has been minced, parsley, dill, chives, and lemon juice should be added. 3. Make sure everything is well blended and smooth. 4. Reduce the amount of time it takes to blend and add salt and pepper according to taste. 5. If you want the taste to blend, put the mixture in a dish and chill it for half an hour before you serve it.

CUCUMBER AVOCADO SALAD

Total Time: 15 minutes | Prep Time: 10 minutes

Ingredients:

1 large cucumber, peeled and diced	1 ripe avocado, diced
1/4 red onion, finely chopped	1/4 cup fresh cilantro, chopped
2 tablespoons lime juice	Salt and pepper to taste

Directions:

1. The diced cucumber, avocado, red onion, and cilantro should be added to the Cuisinart Food Processor. 2. To blend the ingredients without completely pureeing them, pulse them a few times. 3. Salt and pepper should be added after the lime juice has been drizzled in a drizzle. 4. Pulse everything together in a gentle manner, making sure that the avocado maintains its chunky consistency. 5. Place in a dish designed for serving and serve immediately; alternatively, refrigerate for a brief period of time before serving.

OLIVE TAPENADE

Total Time: 10 minutes | Prep Time: 5 minutes

Ingredients:

1 cup pitted olives (black, green, or a mix)	2 tablespoons capers, drained
2 cloves garlic, minced	1/4 cup fresh parsley, chopped
2 tablespoons olive oil	1 tablespoon lemon juice
Pepper to taste	

Directions:

1. The olives, capers, garlic, and parsley should be mixed together in the Cuisinart Food Processor together. 2. While taking care not to overprocess, pulse the ingredients until they are finely chopped. 3. Following the addition of the

lemon juice and olive oil, season the dish with pepper to taste. 4. Proceed to pulse the mixture a few more times until it is thoroughly blended but still has a tiny chunkiness to it. 5. Serve the mixture with crackers or toast after transferring it to a serving platter.

ROASTED RED PEPPER SAUCE

Total Time: 20 minutes | Prep Time: 10 minutes

Ingredients:

1 cup roasted red peppers	1/2 cup heavy cream
2 tablespoons olive oil	2 cloves garlic, minced
1 teaspoon Italian seasoning	Salt and pepper to taste

Directions:

1. Combine the roasted red peppers, heavy cream, olive oil, garlic, and Italian seasoning in the Cuisinart Food Processor. Process until desired consistency is reached. 2. Until the mixture reaches a velvety consistency. 3. Toss in some salt and pepper, then stir to combine a little. 4. Moving the mixture to a small saucepan, reheat it over medium-low heat until it's fully incorporated. 5. Serve as a dipping sauce, on top of spaghetti, or on chicken that has been grilled.

BLUEBERRY ALMOND BALLS

Total Time: 20 minutes | Prep Time: 15 minutes

Ingredients:

1 cup almonds	1 cup pitted dates
1 cup dried blueberries	1 teaspoon vanilla extract
Pinch of salt	Shredded coconut (for rolling)

Directions:

1. Prepare the almonds by pulsing them in the Cuisinart food processor until they are coarsely chopped. 2. Dates, dried blueberries, vanilla essence, and salt should be added to the mixture.

Combine all of the ingredients and pulse until sticky and well combined. 3. Form the mixture into balls by scooping out sections of it that are about the size of a tablespoon. 4. Each ball should be coated by rolling it in crushed coconut. 5. Put the blueberry almond balls on a baking sheet, and then place them in the refrigerator for five minutes so that they may harden. 6. It can be served either cold or at room temperature.

HERBED BUTTER

Total Time: 10 minutes | Prep Time: 10 minutes

Ingredients:

1 cup unsalted butter, softened	2 tablespoons fresh parsley, chopped
2 tablespoons fresh chives, chopped	1 tablespoon fresh thyme, chopped
1 teaspoon garlic powder	Salt and pepper to taste

Directions:

1. Introduce the butter and herbs that have been softened into the Cuisinart food processor. 2. The bowl should be seasoned with garlic powder, salt, and pepper. 3. Process the ingredients until they are completely smooth and well blended. 4. Taste the seasoning, then make any required adjustments. 5. Wrap the herb-seasoned butter in plastic or parchment paper and move it to a baking dish. 6. Form into a log and place in the refrigerator until it becomes solid. 7. To serve on bread, veggies, or meat, slice at the appropriate intervals.

BERRY ALMOND BALLS

Total Time: 20 minutes | Prep Time: 15 minutes

Ingredients:

1 cup almonds	1 cup mixed dried berries (cranberries, blueberries, raspberries)
1 tablespoon honey or maple syrup	1 teaspoon vanilla extract

Pinch of salt
Chopped nuts or seeds (for rolling)

Directions:

1. Using the Cuisinart food processor, place the almonds in the bowl and pulse them until they are finely chopped. 2. Incorporate the dried berries in a mixture of honey or maple syrup, vanilla essence, and salt into the mixture. Pulse until everything is well blended. 3. Take parts of the mixture that are about the size of a tablespoon and shape them into balls. 4. Coat each ball by rolling it in a mixture of chopped nuts or seeds. 5. In order to firm it up, arrange it on a baking sheet and place it in the refrigerator for five minutes. 6. Serve as a sweet or a snack that is high in nutrients.

LEMON CASHEW BARS

Total Time: 1 hour | Prep Time: 20 minutes

Ingredients:

1 cup raw cashews	1 cup pitted dates
1/4 cup lemon juice	Zest of 1 lemon
1/4 cup coconut flour	Pinch of salt

Directions:

1. Make sure the cashews are completely crushed up by blending them in the Cuisinart food processor. 2. Dates that have been pitted, lemon juice, lemon zest, coconut flour, and salt should be added. Be sure to process the mixture until it becomes sticky and thoroughly uniform. 3. Arrange parchment paper in a square baking dish and set it aside. 4. You should press the mixture into the bottom of the dish evenly. 5. Allow it to chill for forty minutes in order to firm up. 6. Cut into bars and serve cold when they have been cooled.

AVOCADO HERB DIP

Total Time: 10 minutes | Prep Time: 10 minutes

Ingredients:

2 ripe avocados	1 cup Greek yogurt
2 tablespoons fresh lime juice	1/4 cup fresh cilantro, chopped
1/4 cup green onions, chopped	Salt and pepper to taste

Directions:

1. After removing the pit from the avocados, cut them in half lengthwise, and then scoop the flesh into the Cuisinart food processor. 2. Mince the cilantro, green onions, lime juice, Greek yogurt, and whatever flavors you choose. 3. Until the resulting mixture is creamy and silky. 4. Take a taste, and if necessary, adjust the seasoning. 5. Place the dip in a bowl designed for serving, and then place it in the refrigerator for a few minutes before serving. 6. You may serve this with chips or fresh veggies.

BASIL MINT CHUTNEY

Total Time: 15 minutes | Prep Time: 15 minutes

Ingredients:

1 cup fresh basil leaves	1/2 cup fresh mint leaves
1/4 cup almonds	2 tablespoons lime juice
1 teaspoon honey	Salt to taste

Directions:

1. Blend the almonds, basil, and mint together in the food processor that you have from Cuisinart. 2. Honey, lime juice, and salt should be added. 3. The mixture should be processed until it is finely chopped and well combined. 4. Test the seasoning, then make any required adjustments. 5. After transferring the chutney to a bowl, leave it to sit for a few minutes so that the flavors may combine. 6. This can be served as a dip, with sandwiches, or with grilled meats.

CHUNKY VEGETABLE SAUCE

Total Time: 1 hour | Prep Time: 20 minutes

Ingredients:

2 tablespoons olive oil	1 onion, diced

2 cloves garlic, minced

1 zucchini, diced

1 can (28 ounces) crushed tomatoes

1 teaspoon dried basil

Fresh basil for garnish (optional)

1 carrot, diced

1 bell pepper, diced

1 teaspoon dried oregano

Salt and pepper to taste

Directions:

1. Prepare the onion and garlic by chopping them in a Cuisinart Food Processor until they are finely chopped. 2. The olive oil should be heated at a medium-high temperature in a big saucepan. When the onion and garlic have become translucent, add them to the pan. 3. Include the carrot, zucchini, and bell pepper that have been diced. 4. Cook the veggies for around five to seven minutes or until they reach the desired tenderness. 5. Mix the crushed tomatoes, oregano, and basil together in a saucepan. To season the meal, use pepper and salt. 6. Simmer for half an hour, stirring the mixture regularly so that the flavors may mingle. 7. As a dipping sauce for bread or as a warm topping for pasta, if desired. 8. If you so want, garnish with some fresh basil.

MATCHA DATE BALLS

Total Time: 15 minutes | Prep Time: 10 minutes

Ingredients:

1 cup pitted dates

2 tablespoons matcha powder

1/2 teaspoon vanilla extract

Unsweetened shredded coconut (for rolling)

1 cup nuts (almonds, walnuts, or cashews)

1 tablespoon coconut oil

Pinch of salt

Directions:

1. Put the dates that have been pitted, the nuts, the matcha powder, the coconut oil, the vanilla essence, and the salt into a Cuisinart Food Processor processor. 2. Put the mixture through a series of pulses until it is finely chopped and begins to clump together. 3. You should scoop out little bits and then use your hands to roll them into balls. 4. Each ball should be coated by rolling it in crushed coconut. 5. After placing the matcha date balls on a dish, place them in the refrigerator for approximately ten minutes so that they may become more solid. 6. Eat cold as a snack or to give yourself a boost of energy. 7. Seal any remaining food in an airtight container and store it in the fridge.

WHITE BEAN GARLIC DIP

Total Time: 10 minutes | Prep Time: 5 minutes

Ingredients:

1 can (15 ounces) white beans, drained and rinsed

2 tablespoons lemon juice

Salt and pepper to taste

2 cloves garlic, minced

3 tablespoons olive oil

Fresh parsley for garnish (optional)

Directions:

1. Blend white beans, garlic, lemon juice, and olive oil in the Cuisinart Food Processor. 2. The mixture should be processed until it is smooth, with the sides being scraped down as necessary. 3. If preferred, add salt and pepper and blend again until combined. 4. Scatter olive oil over the dip in a serving basin. 5. When using fresh parsley, garnish the dish with it. 6. Pita chips or veggie sticks should be served alongside. 7. Refrigerate any leftovers after putting them in an airtight container.

CHOCOLATE COCONUT BITES

Total Time: 15 minutes | Prep Time: 10 minutes

Ingredients:

1 cup pitted dates	1 cup nuts (almonds or cashews)
1/2 cup unsweetened cocoa powder	1/4 cup shredded coconut
1 tablespoon coconut oil	Pinch of salt
Optional: additional shredded coconut for rolling	

Directions:

1. The dates that have been pitted, the almonds, the cocoa powder, the shredded coconut, the coconut oil, and the salt should be mixed together in a Cuisinart Food Processor. 2. Repeat the process until the ingredients are well mixed together and begin to bind together. 3. Make portions by scooping them out and then rolling them into balls with your hands. 4. In order to coat the balls, you might choose to roll them in additional shredded coconut. 5. After placing the chocolate coconut bits on a dish, place them in the refrigerator for approximately five minutes so that they may become more solid. 6. Use it as a delicious treat or snack for your guests. 7. Refrigerate leftovers in a container.

TOMATO BASIL RELISH

Total Time: 30 minutes | Prep Time: 15 minutes

Ingredients:

4 medium tomatoes, chopped	1 cup fresh basil leaves
1/4 cup red onion, finely chopped	2 tablespoons olive oil
1 tablespoon balsamic vinegar	Salt and pepper to taste

Directions:

1. It is recommended that you place the diced tomatoes, basil leaves, and red onion into the Cuisinart food processor. Pulse until extremely finely minced. 2. You should incorporate balsamic vinegar and olive oil into the mixture. Perform a couple more pulses in order to blend. 3. To achieve a complete mixing, season with salt and pepper before pounding again. 4. The relish should be placed in a dish and left for 15 minutes to blend flavors. 5. Served with crackers, grilled meats, or as a topping for bruschetta, this condiment is delicious.

COCONUT MACADAMIA BARS

Total Time: 45 minutes | Prep Time: 15 minutes

Ingredients:

1 cup pitted dates	1 cup raw macadamia nuts
1 cup shredded coconut (unsweetened)	1/4 cup almond flour
1/4 cup honey or maple syrup	1/2 teaspoon vanilla extract
Pinch of salt	

Directions:

1. The macadamia nuts and dates that have been pitted should be mixed together in the Cuisinart food processor. The mixture should be crumbly after being pulsed. 2. Honey, vanilla essence, shredded coconut, almond flour, and salt should be added to the mixture. The mixture should be thoroughly mixed and sticky. 3. Using parchment paper, line a baking dish that is 8 inches by 8 inches. Put the mixture into the dish and press it down evenly. 4. Allow it to chill in the refrigerator for at least half an hour to set. 5. Cut and store bars in an airtight container before refrigerating.

CHOCOLATE COCONUT BLISS BARS

Total Time: 45 minutes | Prep Time: 15 minutes

Ingredients:

1 cup pitted dates	1 cup shredded coconut (unsweetened)

1/2 cup almond flour	1/4 cup cocoa powder
1/4 cup coconut oil, melted	1/4 cup maple syrup
Pinch of salt	

Directions:

1. Put the dates that have been pitted into the Cuisinart food processor and pulse them until they transform into a paste. 2. Include the shredded coconut, almond flour, cocoa powder, maple syrup, and salt in the mixture. Also, include the melted coconut oil. Blend until it is completely smooth. 3. After lining a baking dish of 8 inches by 8 inches with parchment paper, press the mixture into the dish in a uniform manner. 4. Refrigerate for half an hour so that it can be set. 5. Squares should be cut and served either cold at room temperature or chilled.

CHOCOLATE PEPPERMINT BALLS

Total Time: 30 minutes | Prep Time: 15 minutes

Ingredients:

1 cup pitted dates	1/2 cup almond flour
1/4 cup cocoa powder	1/4 cup shredded coconut (unsweetened)
1/4 teaspoon peppermint extract	Pinch of salt
Extra cocoa powder or shredded coconut for rolling	

Directions:

1. The dates that have been pitted, almond flour, cocoa powder, shredded coconut, peppermint essence, and salt should be mixed together in the Cuisinart food processor. Keep blending until sticky and well mixed. 2. Scoop out amounts that are about the size of a tablespoon and shape them into balls. 3. To ensure that the balls are evenly coated, roll them in additional cocoa powder or shredded coconut. 4. After placing the balls on a dish or tray, place them in the refrigerator for fifteen minutes so that they may become more solid. 5. Ensure that the container is sealed and place it in the refrigerator.

GINGERBREAD BALLS

Total Time: 30 minutes | Prep Time: 15 minutes

Ingredients:

1 cup pitted dates	1 cup almond flour
1 teaspoon ground ginger	1 teaspoon cinnamon
1/4 teaspoon nutmeg	1/4 cup molasses
Pinch of salt	1/2 cup crushed nuts or coconut for rolling

Directions:

1. The Cuisinart food processor should be used to combine the dates that have been pitted, almond flour, ground ginger, cinnamon, nutmeg, molasses, and salt. Blend until it is completely smooth. 2. Scoop out amounts that are about the size of a tablespoon and shape them into balls. 3. In order to properly coat the balls, roll them in either crushed nuts or shredded coconut. 4. To allow the mixture to solidify, place it on a dish or tray and place it in the refrigerator for fifteen minutes. 5. You may either keep it in the refrigerator or at room temperature if you store it in an airtight container.

MINT CHIP BITES

Total Time: 30 minutes | Prep Time: 15 minutes

Ingredients:

1 cup almond flour	1 cup Medjool dates, pitted
1/4 cup cocoa powder	1/4 cup unsweetened shredded coconut
1/4 teaspoon peppermint extract	1/4 cup dark chocolate chips

Directions:

1. Put the almond flour, dates, cocoa powder, shredded coconut, and peppermint essence into the Cuisinart food processor and mix them together. 2. Be sure to process the mixture until it becomes sticky and thoroughly uniform. 3. Scoop out amounts that are about the size of a tablespoon and shape them into balls. Place them on a parchment-lined baking sheet. 4. The dark chocolate chips should be melted in a bowl that is safe for the microwave in increments of thirty seconds, with stirring in between each melting. 5. Return each ball to the baking sheet after dipping it in the melted chocolate and ensuring that it is completely covered in the chocolate. 6. Place in the refrigerator for approximately fifteen minutes or until the chocolate has hardened. Eat your mint chip bits with pleasure!

PISTACHIO DATE BARS

Total Time: 45 minutes | Prep Time: 15 minutes

Ingredients:

1 cup Medjool dates, pitted	1 cup raw pistachios
1/2 cup almond flour	1/4 teaspoon sea salt
1 teaspoon vanilla extract	1/4 cup honey (optional)

Directions:

1. Pulse the pistachios in the Cuisinart food processor until they are finely minced for the topping; set aside about two teaspoons. 2. Honey, almond flour, sea salt, vanilla essence, and dates should be added to the food processor. Maintain the blending process until the mixture becomes sticky and well combined. 3. Using parchment paper, line a baking dish that is 8 inches by 8 inches. The mixture should be pressed strongly into the plate in order to create a uniform coating. 4. The pistachios that were set aside should be sprinkled on top and then gently pressed down. 5. Set aside in the refrigerator for at least half an hour, and then cut into bars. It is best to store it in the refrigerator so that it can maintain its freshness.

MUSHROOM WALNUT PÂTÉ

Total Time: 20 minutes | Prep Time: 10 minutes

Ingredients:

2 cups mushrooms, chopped	1 cup walnuts, toasted
2 cloves garlic, minced	2 tablespoons olive oil
1 tablespoon soy sauce	Salt and pepper to taste
Fresh herbs (like thyme or parsley)	

Directions:

1. Put the mushrooms, walnuts, garlic, olive oil, and soy sauce into the Cuisinart food processor. Process until everything is combined. 2. The mixture should be coarsely minced but should still have some texture after being pulsed. 3. The components should be seasoned with salt and pepper to taste, and then they should be pulsed together one more time. 4. Make sure the top is smooth before transferring to a serving dish. Add some fresh herbs as a garnish. 5. Crackers or fresh veggies should be served alongside. Have fun!

CLASSIC COLESLAW

Total Time: 15 minutes | Prep Time: 10 minutes

Ingredients:

4 cups green cabbage, shredded	1 cup carrots, shredded
1/2 cup mayonnaise	2 tablespoons apple cider vinegar
1 tablespoon sugar	Salt and pepper to taste

Directions:

1. Place the cabbage and carrots in the Cuisinart food processor and mix until blended. Pulse until

the mixture is finely shredded. 2. Mayonnaise, apple cider vinegar, sugar, salt, and pepper should be combined in a big basin and stirred together. 3. Include the carrots and cabbage that have been shredded in the bowl. In order to blend, thoroughly mix. 4. Before serving, place the dish in the refrigerator for at least ten minutes to enable the flavors to combine. 5. Prepare as a side dish and serve cold. Let your coleslaw be enjoyed!

BEET AND GOAT CHEESE SALAD

Total Time: 30 minutes | Prep Time: 15 minutes

Ingredients:

2 cups cooked beets, sliced	4 cups mixed greens (like arugula or spinach)
1/2 cup goat cheese, crumbled	1/4 cup walnuts, toasted
2 tablespoons balsamic vinaigrette	Salt and pepper to taste

Directions:

1. Pulse the walnuts in the Cuisinart food processor until they are roughly chopped before proceeding. 2. Prepare the salad by combining the sliced beets, mixed greens, and walnuts in a large bowl. 3. Toss the salad gently to coat it with the balsamic vinaigrette after drizzling it. 4. Salt and pepper should be used to season the goat cheese crumbles that are placed on top. 5. Please serve it immediately as a refreshing salad. Have fun!

GINGER APRICOT BALLS

Total Time: 20 minutes | Prep Time: 20 minutes

Ingredients:

1 cup dried apricots	1 cup almond meal
1/2 cup shredded coconut	1/4 cup honey or maple syrup
1 teaspoon ground ginger	1/2 teaspoon cinnamon
Pinch of salt	

Directions:

1. The dried apricots, almond meal, shredded coconut, honey, crushed ginger, cinnamon, and salt should all be mixed together in the food processor together. 2. After pulsing the ingredients together, you should get a sticky dough. Whenever it is necessary, scrape down the sides. 3. After mixing the ingredients, shape the dough into one-inch balls using your hands. 4. You can choose to roll each ball in more shredded coconut if you so wish. 5. To harden, set the balls on a parchment-lined baking sheet and refrigerate for 30 minutes. 6. Serve cold or at room temperature, whichever you choose. The refrigerator should be used to store the food in an airtight container.

MATCHA GREEN TEA BALLS

Total Time: 15 minutes | Prep Time: 15 minutes

Ingredients:

1 cup pitted dates	1 cup cashews
2 tablespoons matcha green tea powder	1 tablespoon coconut oil
1/2 teaspoon vanilla extract	Pinch of sea salt
Additional coconut for rolling (optional)	

Directions:

1. Place the cashews and dates that have been pitted into the food processor and pulse until they are finely minced. 2. Matcha powder, coconut oil, vanilla essence, and salt from the sea should be added. Continuously process the mixture until it becomes sticky and can be held together. 3. Make the mixture into little balls by using your hands to shape it first. 4. If you want to add some more flavor to the balls, you may roll them in shredded coconut. 5. After placing the balls on a dish, place them in the refrigerator for

at least fifteen minutes so that they may harden. 6. Consume as a nutritious snack time. Ensure that the container is sealed and place it in the refrigerator.

SPICY RED PEPPER TAPENADE

Total Time: 10 minutes | Prep Time: 10 minutes

Ingredients:

1 cup roasted red peppers, drained	1/2 cup pitted black olives
1/4 cup capers, rinsed	2 cloves garlic
2 tablespoons olive oil	1 tablespoon balsamic vinegar
1/2 teaspoon crushed red pepper flakes	

Directions:

1. Roasted red peppers, black olives, capers, and garlic should be mixed together in a food processor. Pulse until the mixture is roughly chopped. 2. After cleaning the bowl, add olive oil, balsamic vinegar, and crushed red pepper flakes. 3. The mixture should be processed once more until it is well mixed but still has some texture. 4. Take a taste, and make any necessary adjustments to the seasoning. 5. Transfer the tapenade to a bowl that can be used for serving, and place it in the refrigerator for at least half an hour before serving so that the flavors may combine. 6. You may serve this dish with bread, crackers, or veggie sticks.

ORANGE GINGER BALLS

Total Time: 20 minutes | Prep Time: 20 minutes

Ingredients:

1 cup dried apricots	1 cup walnuts
Zest of 1 orange	1 tablespoon freshly grated ginger
1 tablespoon maple syrup	1/4 teaspoon cinnamon
Pinch of salt	

Directions:

1. Put the walnuts and dried apricots into the food processor and mix them together. Pulse until extremely finely minced. 2. Include the following ingredients in the mixture: grated ginger, orange zest, maple syrup, cinnamon, and salt. Mix until everything is included. 3. Make little balls with your hands, each measuring approximately one inch in diameter. 4. The balls should be placed on a baking sheet or plate that has been lined with parchment paper. 5. Serve after 30 minutes of refrigeration. 6. It stays fresher in an airtight container in the fridge.

LEMON PECAN BALLS

Total Time: 15 minutes | Prep Time: 15 minutes

Ingredients:

1 cup pecans	1 cup pitted dates
Zest of 1 lemon	2 tablespoons lemon juice
1 teaspoon vanilla extract	Pinch of salt
Additional powdered sugar for rolling (optional)	

Directions:

1. The pecans and dates should be mixed together in the food processor. Combine the ingredients and process them until they are finely chopped and begin to clump together. 2. Include the zest of a lemon, the juice of a lemon, vanilla essence, and salt. Blend until everything is well blended. 3. In order to shape the mixture into little balls, you should use your hands. 4. For a delicious ending, you can choose to roll the balls in powdered sugar if you so wish. 5. At least fifteen minutes should be spent in the refrigerator after placing the balls on a platter. 6. As a wonderful snack, you may enjoy it. Ensure that the container is sealed and place it in the refrigerator.

DAIRY-FREE ALFREDO

Total Time: 15 minutes | Prep Time: 10 minutes

Ingredients:

1 cup raw cashews	1 cup unsweetened almond milk
3 tablespoons nutritional yeast	2 tablespoons lemon juice
2 garlic cloves	Salt and pepper to taste
1 tablespoon olive oil (optional)	

Directions:

1. The cashews that have been soaked should be mixed together in the Cuisinart Food Processor along with almond milk, nutritional yeast, lemon juice, garlic, salt, and pepper. 2. Process until the mixture is silky smooth and creamy, scraping down the sides as necessary. 3. Add olive oil for an additional layer of richness, if preferred, and mix once more until it is completely blended. 4. Taste the seasoning, then make any required adjustments. 5. Before serving the sauce over pasta or vegetables, cook it in a skillet over low heat until it is warm.

CINNAMON DATE BALLS

Total Time: 15 minutes | Prep Time: 10 minutes

Ingredients:

1 cup pitted dates	1 cup rolled oats
1 teaspoon cinnamon	1/4 cup almond butter
1/4 cup chopped nuts	Pinch of salt
Shredded coconut (optional for rolling)	

Directions:

1. Place the dates, oats, cinnamon, almond butter, almonds, and salt into the Cuisinart Food Processor and process until everything is combined. 2. The mixture should be well mixed and sticky after being pulsed. 3. Using your moist hands, shape the mixture into little balls approximately one inch in diameter. 4. Should you so wish, you can roll each ball with shredded coconut. 5. When you are ready to serve the date balls, place them on a dish and place them in the refrigerator for at least ten minutes.

ROASTED GARLIC AIOLI

Total Time: 20 minutes | Prep Time: 10 minutes

Ingredients:

1 head of garlic	1 cup mayonnaise (dairy-free if needed)
1 tablespoon lemon juice	Salt and pepper to taste
Olive oil (optional for consistency)	

Directions:

1. Bake at 400°F. After removing the top of the head of garlic, sprinkle it with olive oil, wrap it in aluminum foil, and roast it for around twenty minutes until it becomes tender. 2. When the garlic has reached room temperature, remove the cloves that have been roasted and place them in the Cuisinart Food Processor. 3. A mixture of mayonnaise, lemon juice, salt, and pepper should be added. 4. Perform the processing until the mixture is silky smooth and creamy, correcting the consistency with olive oil if necessary. 5. Wraps, sandwiches, or veggies can be served with this dip or spread.

VANILLA BERRY BALLS

Total Time: 15 minutes | Prep Time: 10 minutes

Ingredients:

1 cup rolled oats	1/2 cup almond butter
1/2 cup dried mixed berries (cranberries, blueberries, etc.)	1 teaspoon vanilla extract
1 tablespoon honey or maple syrup (optional)	Pinch of salt

1. Rolling oats, almond butter, dried berries, vanilla essence, honey, and salt should be mixed together in the Cuisinart Food Processor after being combined. 2. The mixture should be processed until it is of a sticky consistency and holds together. 3. To make balls, scoop out pieces and roll them into balls with a diameter of about one inch. 4. Arrange the balls in a single layer on a dish or baking sheet. 5. Before serving, place the mixture in the refrigerator for approximately ten minutes on high.

MATCHA ALMOND BARS

Total Time: 25 minutes | Prep Time: 15 minutes

Ingredients:

1 cup almonds	1/2 cup almond flour
1/4 cup maple syrup	2 tablespoons matcha powder
1/4 teaspoon salt	1 teaspoon vanilla extract

Directions:

1. Mix the almonds and almond flour together in the Cuisinart Food Processor, and then pulse the mixture until it is completely ground. 2. Incorporate matcha powder, maple syrup, salt, and vanilla essence into the mixture. 3. Continue processing the ingredients until they form a dough that is sticky and cohesive. 4. Press dough evenly into an 8-by-8-inch parchment-lined baking dish. 5. Before cutting into bars, allow the mixture to set in the refrigerator for at least ten minutes.

SMOKY BLACK BEAN SALSA

Total Time: 15 minutes | Prep Time: 15 minutes

Ingredients:

1 can (15 oz) black beans	1 medium tomato, diced
1/4 cup red onion, finely chopped	1 jalapeño pepper, seeded and chopped
1/4 cup fresh cilantro, chopped	1 lime, juiced
1 teaspoon smoked paprika	Salt and pepper to taste

Directions:

1. Using the Cuisinart Food Processor, blend the following Ingredients: black beans, tomato, red onion, jalapeño, and cilantro. 2. Pulse the items until they are roughly chopped and distributed evenly. 3. Include smoked paprika, lime juice, salt, and pepper in the mixture. 4. Again, pulse to integrate the flavors; however, do not overprocess the mixture. 5. Test the seasoning, then make any required adjustments. 6. Serve while still warm with tortilla chips, or store in the refrigerator for up to two days.

PUMPKIN SPICE SOUP

Total Time: 30 minutes | Prep Time: 10 minutes

Ingredients:

1 tablespoon olive oil	1 onion, chopped
2 cloves garlic, minced	1 can (15 oz) pumpkin puree
3 cups vegetable broth	1 teaspoon pumpkin pie spice
1/2 cup coconut milk	Salt and pepper to taste

Directions:

1. Oil a large saucepan and set it over medium heat to warm. When the onion and garlic become a pale yellow, toss them in. 2. Stir in the pumpkin pie spice, vegetable broth, and pureed pumpkin. 3. Simmer, covered, for about 10 minutes on low heat. 4. Put the soup in the food processor and process until it's completely smooth. 5. Put the pureed soup back into the saucepan and mix in the coconut milk. 6. After heating, add salt and pepper to taste. 7. While still hot, top it with a little coconut milk if you want.

ROASTED EGGPLANT SPREAD

Total Time: 45 minutes | Prep Time: 15 minutes

Ingredients:

1 medium eggplant, halved	2 cloves garlic, unpeeled
2 tablespoons tahini	2 tablespoons lemon juice
1 tablespoon olive oil	Salt and pepper to taste
Fresh parsley for garnish	

Directions:

1. The oven should be 400°F or 200°C. 2. On a baking sheet, spread the garlic and half of the eggplant. 3. Roast, drizzling with olive oil, for 30–35 minutes or until tender. 4. Take it out of the oven and allow it to cool for a little. Peel the garlic and remove the meat from the eggplant. 5. Mash the garlic, and add the tahini, lemon juice, salt, and pepper to the Cuisinart Food Processor with the eggplant flesh. 6. While blending, taste and add more spice if needed. 7. Place in a serving dish and top with chopped parsley. 8. Accompany with pita bread and veggie sticks.

CLASSIC MAYONNAISE

Total Time: 10 minutes | Prep Time: 5 minutes

Ingredients:

1 large egg	1 tablespoon Dijon mustard
1 tablespoon white vinegar	1 cup vegetable oil
Salt to taste	

Directions:

1. The egg, Dijon mustard, and vinegar should be mixed together in the Cuisinart Food Processor. 2. Blend at a high speed until everything is well combined. 3. While the food processor is operating, gradually add the vegetable oil from a trickle. 4. Maintain the blending process until the mixture becomes more viscous and emulsifies. 5. Add salt to taste, then process for a few seconds to incorporate the ingredients. 6. The

combination can be refrigerated for a week in a clean container. 7. Utilize as a spread, as well as in salads and dressings alike.

CASHEW CREAM

Total Time: 10 minutes | Prep Time: 10 minutes (soak time not included)

Ingredients:

1 cup raw cashews, soaked in water	1/4 cup water (more for desired consistency)
1 tablespoon lemon juice	Salt to taste

Directions:

1. The cashews that have been soaked should be drained and rinsed before being placed in the Cuisinart Food Processor. 2. Salt, water, and lemon juice should be added. 3. Scrape down the edges as needed to blend until smooth and creamy. 4. If you want the consistency to be thinner, adjust the water accordingly. 5. Perform a taste test and, if required, add additional salt or lemon juice. 6. You may use this ingredient as a dairy-free alternative in recipes or as a topping for foods. 7. You may keep it in the refrigerator for up to five days if you store it in an airtight container.

ALMOND COCONUT BARS

Total Time: 1 hour | Prep Time: 20 minutes

Ingredients:

1 cup almonds	1 cup unsweetened shredded coconut
1/2 cup honey or maple syrup	1/4 cup coconut oil, melted
1/2 teaspoon vanilla extract	1/4 teaspoon salt

Directions:

1. Place parchment paper in an 8x8-inch baking dish and preheat to 350°F/175°C. 2. Chop the almonds finely in the Cuisinart Food Processor

by pulsing them. 3. Honey, coconut oil, salt, vanilla essence, and shredded coconut should be added. To make a sticky mixture, process until all ingredients are well incorporated. 4. Use all your force to push the mixture evenly into the baking dish you have prepared. 5. Preheat the oven to 300 degrees and brown the top by baking it for 30–40 minutes. 6. Cut into bars once they have cooled entirely in the pan. 7. Keep in the fridge for up to a week if sealed tightly.

COFFEE HAZELNUT BALLS

Total Time: 30 minutes | Prep Time: 15 minutes

Ingredients:

1 cup hazelnuts	1/2 cup pitted dates
1/4 cup brewed coffee, cooled	1 tablespoon cocoa powder
1/2 teaspoon vanilla extract	Pinch of salt

Directions:

1. Chop the hazelnuts finely in a Cuisinart food processor, but do not process until they become nut butter. 2. Be sure to include salt, cocoa powder, boiled coffee, pitted dates, and vanilla essence. All of the ingredients should be mixed together until a sticky dough is formed. 3. A little extra coffee can be added if the mixture seems too dry. 4. Shape the dough into little balls, each approximately one inch in diameter. 5. Assemble the balls on a baking sheet that has been lined with parchment paper. 6. To set, give it a 15-minute chill in the fridge. 7. Refrigerate for a maximum of two weeks if stored in an airtight container.

CINNAMON RAISIN BALLS

Total Time: 25 minutes | Prep Time: 10 minutes

Ingredients:

1 cup rolled oats	1/2 cup raisins
1/4 cup almond butter	1 tablespoon honey
1 teaspoon cinnamon	Pinch of salt

Directions:

1. The rolled oats should be pulsed in the Cuisinart Food Processor until they are ground to a very fine consistency. 2. The raisins, almond butter, honey, cinnamon, and salt should be added at this point. Ensure that the material is well mixed by processing it. 3. You may need to add a little water to the mixture in order to bring it together if it is too dry. 4. Assemble the ingredients into little balls with a diameter of approximately one inch. 5. On a dish, arrange the balls, and then place them in the refrigerator for fifteen minutes to chill. 6. As soon as possible, consume or keep it in an airtight container. 7. A week is the maximum amount of time that they may be stored in the refrigerator.

LEMON BASIL AIOLI

Total Time: 10 minutes | Prep Time: 10 minutes

Ingredients:

1 cup mayonnaise	2 tablespoons fresh lemon juice
2 cloves garlic, minced	1/4 cup fresh basil leaves
Salt and pepper to taste	

Directions:

1. Toss the basil leaves, mayonnaise, lemon juice, and minced garlic in a Cuisinart food processor. 2. Blend and process the ingredients until they are completely combined. 3. Salt & pepper to taste. 4. Extra lemon juice can be used for a thinner consistency. 5. Put in the fridge for 30 minutes before serving after transferring to a serving dish. 6. Dip vegetables in it or use it as a spread on sandwiches. 7. Put any leftovers in a sealed container and store them in the fridge for no more than a week.

BASIL GARLIC BUTTER

Total Time: 10 minutes | Prep Time: 10 minutes

Ingredients:

1 cup unsalted butter, softened	1/4 cup fresh basil leaves
2 cloves garlic, minced	Salt to taste

Directions:

1. Put the melted butter, basil leaves, garlic powder, and salt into the Cuisinart food processor. 2. Pulse the ingredients until they reach a velvety consistency. 3. If needed, taste and make adjustments to the seasoning. 4. Place the butter on a parchment-lined baking sheet. 5. Form a log form by rolling it and twisting the ends to seal it. 6. Let it set in the fridge for at least an hour, preferably longer. 7. Slice and enjoy with a side of veggies or toast, or put it to use in the kitchen. Refrigerate any remaining food for a maximum of two weeks.

LEMON DILL SAUCE

Total Time: 10 minutes | Prep Time: 10 minutes

Ingredients:

1 cup Greek yogurt	2 tablespoons fresh dill, chopped
2 tablespoons fresh lemon juice	1 teaspoon lemon zest
1 clove garlic, minced	Salt and pepper to taste

Directions:

1. Combine the dill, Greek yogurt, lemon zest, lemon juice, and minced garlic in the Cuisinart food processor. 2. Blend or puree the ingredients in a food processor until smooth. 3. To taste, add salt and pepper. 4. After you scrape the bowl's sides, give it another quick pulse to combine. 5. Fill a serving dish or sealable container with the sauce. 6. Put it in the fridge for half an hour to let the flavors combine. 7. Drizzle over cooked chicken or fish, or use as a dip for veggies.

VANILLA OAT BALLS

Total Time: 15 minutes | Prep Time: 10 minutes

Ingredients:

1 cup rolled oats	1/2 cup almond butter
1/4 cup honey or maple syrup	1 teaspoon vanilla extract
1/4 teaspoon salt	1/4 cup mini chocolate chips (optional)

Directions:

1. The rolled oats, almond butter, honey (or maple syrup), vanilla extract, and salt should be mixed together in the Cuisinart Food Processor once it has been processed. 2. While pulsing, scrape down the edges of the bowl as necessary to ensure that the mixture is thoroughly mixed and sticky. 3. Adding the micro chocolate chips and pulsing the mixture a few times will ensure that they are distributed evenly. 4. Your hands should be used to shape the mixture into little balls that are approximately one inch in diameter. 5. It is recommended that the balls be put in a certain pattern on a baking sheet that has been coated with parchment paper. 6. For approximately five minutes, chill the mixture in the refrigerator so that it may become more solid. 7. You may keep it in the refrigerator for up to a week if you store it in an airtight container.

CARROT CAKE BALLS

Total Time: 25 minutes | Prep Time: 15 minutes

Ingredients:

1 cup grated carrots	1 cup rolled oats
1/2 cup walnuts or pecans, chopped	1/2 cup almond flour
1/4 cup maple syrup	1 teaspoon cinnamon
1/4 teaspoon nutmeg	1/4 cup raisins (optional)

Directions:

1. Put the grated carrots, rolled oats, chopped nuts, almond flour, maple syrup, cinnamon, and nutmeg into the Cuisinart Food Processor.

Process until everything is evenly distributed. 2. Pulse the ingredients until they are thoroughly mixed together, and the product is able to keep its shape. 3. The raisins, if used, should be added and then pulsed a few times to spread them. 4. Your hands should be used to shape the mixture into little balls that are approximately one inch in diameter. 5. Line a parchment paper-lined baking sheet with the carrot cake balls. 6. To get the desired consistency, place the mixture in the refrigerator for approximately ten minutes. 7. You may keep it in the refrigerator for up to a week if you store it in an airtight container.

BLACK BEAN QUESO

Total Time: 15 minutes | Prep Time: 15 minutes

Ingredients:

1 can (15 oz) black beans	1 cup shredded cheddar cheese
1 cup salsa	1/2 cup cream cheese, softened
1 teaspoon cumin	1 teaspoon chili powder
1/2 teaspoon garlic powder	Salt and pepper to taste
Fresh cilantro for garnish (optional)	

Directions:

1. Black beans, cheddar cheese, salsa, cream cheese, cumin, chili powder, garlic powder, salt, and pepper should be combined in the Cuisinart Food Processor. 2. Pulse the ingredients until they are thoroughly incorporated but still have a somewhat chunky consistency for texture. 3. Test the seasoning, then make any required adjustments. 4. Put the queso in a bowl that is suitable for serving. 5. In the event that you so wish, garnish with fresh cilantro and serve with tortilla chips.

BERRY BLISS BALLS

Total Time: 20 minutes | Prep Time: 20 minutes

Ingredients:

1 cup mixed berries (fresh or frozen)	1 cup oats
1/2 cup almond butter	1/4 cup honey or maple syrup
1/4 cup shredded coconut	1 teaspoon vanilla extract
Pinch of salt	

Directions:

1. After adding the mixed berries to the Cuisinart Food Processor, pulse the machine until the berries are completely broken down. 2. All of the following ingredients should be added: oats, almond butter, honey (or maple syrup), shredded coconut, vanilla essence, and salt. 3. The mixture should be processed until it is together and sticky. 4. Prepare the mixture by shaping it into little balls with a diameter of approximately one inch using your hands. 5. To harden, set the balls on a parchment-lined baking sheet and refrigerate for 30 minutes.

VANILLA HAZELNUT BARS

Total Time: 25 minutes | Prep Time: 10 minutes

Ingredients:

1 cup hazelnuts, toasted	1 cup pitted dates
1 cup rolled oats	1 teaspoon vanilla extract
1/4 cup almond flour	Pinch of salt
Dark chocolate for drizzling (optional)	

Directions:

1. Using a Cuisinart food processor, combine the roasted hazelnuts with the remaining ingredients and pulse the mixture until it reaches the consistency of a fine powder. 2. Pit the dates and combine them with the rolled oats, salt, almond flour, and vanilla essence. 3. The mixture should be processed until it becomes sticky and

stays put. 4. Pat out a baking dish that measures 8 by 8 inches. 5. The mixture should be pressed down into the bottom of the pan, which has been prepared in an even manner. 6. Set in the fridge for at least 15 minutes. Melt some dark chocolate and pour it over the top; then cut into bars if you like.

MOCHA WALNUT BARS

Total Time: 30 minutes | Prep Time: 15 minutes

Ingredients:

1 cup walnuts	1 cup pitted dates
1/2 cup oats	2 tablespoons cocoa powder
1 tablespoon instant coffee granules	1/4 teaspoon salt

1/4 cup dark chocolate chips (optional)

Directions:

1. With the oven preheated at 350°F (175°C), line an 8x8-inch baking tray with parchment paper. 2. Put everything into the Cuisinart Food Processor: walnuts, pitted dates, oats, cocoa powder, instant coffee, and salt. 3. Mix everything together in a blender until it gets sticky. 4. Evenly distribute the batter into the preheated baking dish. 5. Toss in some dark chocolate chips and press them lightly into the mixture if you're using them. 6. Cut into bars when they have cooled, which should take around 15 minutes after baking.

THE END

Made in United States
Orlando, FL
26 December 2024

56547278R00057